Tee Hammond is an author from Chicago, Illinois. Her past is not pretty but she is committed to change. She is a strong advocate of the LGBTQA+ community she is a part of as a woman of color who is transgender. Contact her as she pays her debt to society. Her info is:

Tee Hammond #M16732
Centralia Correctional Center
P.O. Box 7711
Centralia, IL 62801

To my loved ones, thank you for being patient.

Freckles, you have impacted my life in ways I never imagined.

Chonna and Antoinette, y'all know wassup! I love you to the moon and back.

To the staff at Austin Macauley Publishers, thank you all for giving me a literary home. This has been an amazing experience.

Tee Hammond

STRIPPING

Taking Off Everything to
Love What's Underneath

AUSTIN MACAULEY PUBLISHERS™

LONDON • CAMBRIDGE • NEW YORK • SHARJAH

Ordering Information
Quantity sales: Special discounts are available on quantity purchases by corporations, associations, and others. For details, contact the publisher at the address below.

Publisher's Cataloging-in-Publication data
Hammond, Tee
Stripping

ISBN 9798889107903 (Paperback)
ISBN 9798889107910 (ePub e-book)

Library of Congress Control Number: 2023924425

www.austinmacauley.com/us

First Published 2024
Austin Macauley Publishers LLC
40 Wall Street, 33rd Floor, Suite 3302
New York, NY 10005
USA

mail-usa@austinmacauley.com
+1 (646) 5125767

Lil savage,

"If you make me write one more book, I swear we gonna get into it! Nah, really, you a big part of why I keep going. Love you, shorty!"

March 3rd 2021

Next month, I will be turning twenty-nine. Damn, the last year of my twenties. It doesn't seem that big of a deal. But sometimes I look back to when I was thirteen-ish or fourteen and can remember old people telling me I'd be lucky to see eighteen. They would say, "Keep it up, you gone be dead or in jail."

I wasn't eager to hear that shit, but it turns out that they were half right.

I'm literally writing this from Cellblock 3C in a high-medium/low-maximum security prison.

I'm not proud to be here or of the things I've done that landed me here. I've been "gone" since August 1st, 2017, and am slated for release in February of 2028. A lot of thoughts go through my head regularly, and many things I wish wouldn't come to mind. You wouldn't know it by seeing me, though, because since I learned to strip, I've become a whole different person.

The Start 1992

I was born in Chicago to a mother who put drugs before her kids. I was told I have plenty siblings, but I don't know them. Once our mother lost or relinquished her rights, we were all split up.

I've been told I was nine months old when I was picked by a foster family.

Fast forward to '98, and I was adopted by that same foster family.

Now I had a "new start" and a new name. I was now the youngest of five kids, four of us adopted.

We lived in a decent house on a decent street in the vast suburb of Bolingbrook, Illinois.

There was Chuck, the oldest, Tekela, the second oldest, Ira, the next, and then me.

Our parents were around, but mostly they were at work or church. So, most of the time, the youngest of us four siblings were at home, doing us. As a kid, I didn't realize I was different until I would go outside. Inside the house, I would study Mama and learn the importance of knowing nails, fashion, and matching. When she wasn't around, I would study Tekela, who I call Keke. I learned real style and flair from her and followed her around like she was a real celebrity. I didn't really study my brothers.

There was nothing wrong with me having a stronger connection to females and emulating what I saw. But this was the late nineties/early 2000s. So, before I knew it, I would be teased by kids, whispered about by adults, and talked to by my uncle.

The Talk

Uncle slim wasn't really my uncle. He was my godfather and was hella tight with my dad, who was a deacon at church. It turned out I would have to see him a lot when my dad didn't know what to say to me.

Uncle slim had me, him, and a Bible in his room. He gave me a long speech and a scripture after seeing how I looked at another boy. He told me all about how I can't like boys, how it's not right. At the time, I smiled, nodded, and bowed my head when he prayed, but when I left the room, I still felt exactly how I felt when he called me for our discussion.

Before then, my Aunt Mag would get on me about how "boys don't sit that way," "boys don't walk that way," and so on.

Aunt Maggie was and is one of the toughest people I've ever known. The only lil lady who can make a room of rowdy kids shut up just by counting to three. She is also really my godmother. Out of the three sets of godparents, I liked being at her house the most. Everything smelled like cinnamon there.

I would study her too, but I had to chill, or she'd get into that "Adam is for eve" shit.

At this time, it was unheard of me to say, "Yeah, I know I was born a guy, but I don't feel like one."

As I said before, I didn't feel different till I wasn't at home. The first time I remember being called "Gay and Faggot". I was very young in elementary school. I remember going to Keke with tears in my eyes and telling her what happened, as well as her sticking up for me.

Later on, I would learn to pack away the secret 'cause I felt safest that way back then.

If nobody knew what I liked, nobody could single me out.

It's safe to say most the shit I learned in school didn't come from classes. Mike and Tae was so fuckin' silly, it ain't make no sense. I don't know if Mike Eva told Tae what he suspected, but I wouldn't know 'cause it wasn't long before I got kicked out of Humphrey and stopped to go into school altogether.

Preteen Dropout

Now that I wasn't doin' school, I wanted to do the same for church. I wasn't feelin that shit. I believe people should believe what they want, but as an early teen, I wasn't there for that.

The highlight of going to Alpha for me was listening to the songs, talkin shit with my godbrother, and seeing the women and guys. By now, I liked females a little, but they mostly wouldn't know 'cause I used to be shy when it came to them. This was also one of the only places I went where the girls were finer than the guys to me. Light skin, dark skin, caramel, they all were there!

Now gettin' into so much trouble used to get my ass whooped so much. But the part that blew me the most was that it wasn't my parents who'd whoop us, it was our oldest brother Chuck. At the time, he'd been workin' out hard as fuck and must've been a lil stronger than he thought. Them times were the worst 'cause he hit HARD. Belts hurt, but extension cords would tear the skin off a bitch!

Him being disciplinarian wasn't working, and our bond was strained, like how you a beat the fuck out us then expect us to fuck with you.

Eventually, things came to a head. A sibling put rubbing alcohol into Chuck's tea to try to poison him. It didn't work; Chuck smelled it. The sibling got found out and then sent back to DCFS.

Now it was just Keke, me, Chuck, and the parents. The parents were mostly off. Chuck stopped whoopin' us. Keke was around, but I wasn't. I was out and about looking to see what I could get into.

13

By early '05, I was running away all the time. Nobody knew what to do with me, but I wasn't really doing much when I was sneaking out. I was walking, talking, and dressing like a boy. I didn't have the fancy clothes like in the music videos, but I would go to the stores and peel they ass and bounce. That's how I got my clothes and shoes.

This was cool for a minute, but what was looking good was fast money. Fast money…all of which was quite a way though, so let me slow down a bit.

Around 2001, we moved from our okay house to a big ass house with a lot of space. There was a girl who lived next door, and that was the first girl I really looked at like, "Mmm, she cute." Maybe it was how she looked, maybe it was how she was a tom boy. What I do know is the only person I liked more than her was a boy named Anthony who lived down the street.

Crush

Anthony was so boyish and everything I wasn't, but we got along and got into so much trouble in school. I had the biggest crush on him, and when I was around him, I had butterflies. I didn't know how to him how I felt, and about a year later, I looked up, and his family had moved away.

Playin Str8

Time went on, and in order to not feel so out of place, I would "play straight" at church, which I hated to go to, around my godparents, and at school sometimes. But I guess I wasn't a good enough actor 'cause one day, as a middle schooler, a friend of mine called me out. By now, I'd been kicked out of B.J. Ward and did a while at an alternative school in a different town, where I kissed a guy for the first time. Eventually, I stopped getting in trouble, and the higher-ups figured it was time to go back to regular school. So, shortly after, it was Humphrey, where I was in lunch with Mike and Tae. Tae went off to get something, so Mike and I was sitting there, and there were girls left and right. Mike and Tae was always hitting on the girls, tryna talk to em, and falling for 'em.

I never really pointed one out but would sometimes agree when Mike was goin' on. A girl named Brittany went by, and she was cute, but I wasn't tryin to talk. Next thing I know, Mike is goin' nuts, talkin' shit, "Ahh!! You gay, ain't you!"

I was mortified and denied that shit to the end.

Looking back, I wished I would come clean to my friend, but I didn't tell the truth 'cause I wanted to "fit in".

I didn't really care for classes at Humphrey. It wasn't wild and crazy like at the alternative school, and I also stood out 'cause my clothes weren't the "in" style. There also wasn't any sex for me poppin' there. I wished I was at the old school.

After kissing a guy, I started getting involved with the guys, and soon enough, I had sex with one.

I lost my virginity in the most unromantic fashion. I swear to Gawd; I thought my ass was broken.

The first time I had a nice amount of weed came on a fluke. I would peel the stores for whatever, but one time I took a nice ass MP3 player. I loved music, because it took me away from feeling awkward. Anyway, I had it, and one night I came around some guys I used to go to school with, including Bree. His homies wasn't my homies; I just knew them. When we bumped into each other, it was late, and we started hangin' out. Once we were at his mama's house, he offered me an eight of weed.

I was like, "Show me," and he took me to his older brother's room and showed me his stash.

We ended up back upstairs and were smoking when I tossed it to him like, "Here," since I knew he was good.

As the night went on, I noticed Bree had left without giving me my shit. So, I went down to his brother's room and took what turned out to be three ounces. I never went back over, and, strangely enough, I never ran into Bree again.

I pinched off the ounces to smoke and went around till I got the rest off. I liked having money now. At home, shit was dry as fuck. As of now, I was basically an at-risk youth, and I was barely ever home. Keke and I was, and forever would be, tight, but she was off doin' her own shit.

Bending to the pressure of what people would say, I was carrying shit real boyish, but I wasn't super thuggy. I was more of a pretty boy.

20

06

Summer 06 was poppin' in a crazy way. A lot of firsts went down for me, like the first time I ever spent the night with a girl.

Outside of the girls at church, school, and around the way, I didn't really check for them.

Until here…

Her

Some guys and I were riding around, and the best place we could think of to hang out was Pelican Harbor. Pelican Harbor is a place in the town with a whole lot to do, including a pool.

As usual, the guys had never seen me holler at a girl, even though I would talk shit like I be doin it when they wasn't around. Today, that shit ain't work. So, off of saving face, once we hit the parking lot, I was ready to prove I had game.

The guy who was driving wasn't even my homie; he was just cool with one of my boys. He looked up talkin bout, "What about her?"

I told him to pull up on her, and I hopped out and got her attention. I don't remember what I said. After talkin' for a while, she and I didn't exchange numbers; we decided to dip and hang out. As she walked, I couldn't help but take note of her frame as we left.

Shanquilla was dark-skinned and a lil shorter than me. She was slight and had these lips I couldn't stop looking at. She told me she was fifteen, and that was cool 'cause I was fourteen.

When we got to her house, I met her lil sister, and we went downstairs to her room. Alone.

Kissin and feeding on each other was iight but once we was naked it was whole nother thing.

I wasn't scared, but I didn't know it would go this far, mainly because I only talked to her to save face.

We did a lot, and by the time I left, three days later, it was like, "Okay, so I liked pussy outside of watching porn, and seeing about it a couple times at the alternative school." She was also the first time I ate a pussy.

Our time was short, though, 'cause we was on our way to Beacon Ridge for me to get some money, and just to happen Uncle Slim rode by. I was hopin' he'd keep goin' but it ain't go that way. I knew it and kept walkin' shorty.

Uncle Slim pulled alongside us and wouldn't stop callin' me. When he stopped the car, I got sick to my stomach. At this point, I got in the car 'cause I wasn't tryna get twirled in front of this girl.

Once back at the house, it went down. I was past gettin' whooped, though, and wasn't goin' for anything like it. My Pops turned up on me and I turned all the way up in that bitch. Promptly cussin' him and everyone else out. I knew I went too far when a couple hours later a case worker showed up tryna talk.

Next thing you know I was on the way to Stream Wood Behavioral Health Center for an evaluation. At the time, I thought I'd go in, answer question, and be out, but I was wrong…

Streamwood

I answered all the questions asked. Then they asked why I was acting out. I didn't look at it as acting out; I knew I was acting "straight", but as far as running away and doing a lot, I just looked at it as going to hang out and seeing "what's out there".

Sidebar: Put-ons so far

What I know now is I had put on a few things:

- A "tough" demeanor so I wouldn't be mistaken for "soft" to make up for all the whispers and how I was seen.
- A "boy suit" 'cause I only looked like a boy and acted like one, but didn't feel like one.
- A sharp tongue 'cause cussin' people out usually got me out of conversations I didn't want to have.

Streamwood Part 2

Okay, back to Streamwood… "Streamwood Part 2"

Streamwood was ridiculous for me 'cause here I was, wishing I was at home, looking at a whole bunch of people who were really fucked up. A few was just "bad" like me, but you had voice–hearing, jello–eating, pull prescribed ass people around you all the time here.

A couple day went by, and I started getting antsy, wondering, "Why am I still here?" type shit. I would be told, "Your under observation, usually two weeks, and then you'll be home." So I chilled and took it, till I looked up more than a month later, and I was still there. I was pissed and didn't know what to do. Eventually, I got into a couple of fights. One came from an argument, and the other from a boy I was roomed with who took it upon himself to touch me for his own pleasure just because I was there.

I liked guys, the thing is, though, just cause I liked guys didn't mean all guys. But he ain't need to know that, and I didn't like him or give him permission to fuck with me. When asked why I was fighting, I didn't tell because not snitching was still a thing back then.

I got moved to a different room, but I didn't care about that. I wanted out.

More time went by, and I didn't know what to believe. I had stopped fighting and was being "good", so "Why am I still there?" was my main question when I saw the counselor.

Eventually, I was told that tomorrow I'd be going home. I was happy because it was now November, I'd been there for four months.

The car ride was cool, and my mind was on what I'd be getting into once back in Bolingbrook. We stopped, and the caseworker got us McDonald's, which was way better than the food at Streamwood.

At some point, I fell asleep, and once I woke up, I remember asking how long we had till we got home. I was told we were close, but I didn't see how close 'cause I ain't recognize shit around me.

Once we stopped, I was sure it was a mistake. I asked where we were, and I was told Chicago.
I had a million questions for her before I got out the car.

Turns out I did go too far with all the running away and doing what I wanted. The Hammonds didn't know what to do with me and signed me back over to DCFS. I learned that the reason I was in Streamwood for so long was because they were looking to keep me safe and out of my own way until bedspace was available at this group home we were in front of. I took in what I was told and went through a range of emotions: anger, being upset, feeling tricked. But even when I got sad, I didn't cry 'cause I was taught not to.

Lawrence Hall Youth Services

Once I got in the house, my brave face was on. On the inside, I didn't know how to feel. I had never been in a house with this many guys. It felt like they were picking me apart with they're eyes since I was new. I couldn't act nervous, though. Once I met everybody, I was assigned a room to share with a boy named Twan. Twan was cool, and I met a lot of people outside of the house through him. Meeting new people wasn't really what I was into, but I figured, "This my home now. This my new neighborhood. I gotta fit in." so I went along to get along.

My new family was really just me and seven other teens and preteens in a two-flat on Avers and Carmen. No mamas, no daddies, just staff who worked for Lawrence Hall, who, for the most part, let us do anything "so long as nobody dies."

House Rules

Listen, before I got to Chicago, I thought I was "tough", but when I tell you I had a lot to learn, I had a lot to learn, and fast if I wanted to make it.

- In the house, you had to lookout for yourself.
- In the house, if you was called out, you had to fight.
- If someone takes from you, get it back ASAP.
- If you don't get what's there to eat as soon as it's available, you gonna be hungry.

It was crazy to live this way, but as crazy as we were with each other. We wasn't lettin nobody outside of the house treat us in any kind of way. Not even a lil bit.

I had nothing when I got to the house on Avers—two outfits the Hammond's sent with me to Streamwood, the one I came there in, and a pair of shoes I took from a store back in Bolingbrook.

I was first taken to shop for some clothes and cosmetics.

School, Or Not

Then I was enrolled in school. I hadn't been to school in a looong while, so I didn't really feel it. After going with a staff member to Roosevelt High School and being asked my age, I was told to sit in the office. Shortly after, I was told, "You now in ninth grade," which was news to me 'cause I hadn't completed a grade since sixth. But it was what it was…

Chicago school was waaayyy different than any school I'd ever been to. It was girls everywhere, guys everywhere, and nobody ever seemed to be in class. It was always poppin'. I tried going to classes, but couldn't really keep up because although I was old enough to be a freshman, I wasn't really one work–wise. So I mostly would do something to get kicked out of class, then hang out instead of seeing the principal's office.

Hanging out led to me cutting school, and cutting school led to me stayin out all night, which led to me getting in trouble at the house. Getting "in trouble" was nothing, though. All one of the staff did was write you up and say you can't go out. But that didn't matter because all you had to do was walk back out and come through when you wanted.

The thing was, though, as being a ward of the state, DCFS is liable for you. So when you get wrote up, it goes in your file for being absent without leave or "A.W.O.L." Then if you gone for longer than twenty-four hours, they gotta call the police for a missing person report.

The only thing sucked was that if the police found you out and about and searched you, depending on what was on you, you was goin' to jail. Or if they came across you in general, it could be bad, period, 'cause CPD had some dirty ass police.

If you did run into some who not on dirt, they would just take you to the precinct and wait for the group home to get you, or just drop you off at the home.

It wasn't long before I found myself in real trouble. Through school, I met a guy named Juan.

Juan sold drugs, and he took a likening to me. He was a senior and always had flashy shit on. I liked dressing too, but I wasn't fuckin' with him. Juan would see me watching him, and one day he approached me, asking if I smoked. I told him I didn't, but I did ask him how I could make some money since he seemed to have a lot of it.

He asked if I was in a gang, and I told him no. Then he wanted to know if I knew about the gang he was in. I knew, but I told him I ain't into that and how I just needed to have a way to make money.

After a while, I was banging packs for Juan, but I wasn't making enough to get on my own.

How much I got paid was based on how much I sold, so I would go hard so my pay would be sumthin' slight.

One day, I was skipping class and had a few sales left to make. I was on the bottom floor of the three-floor school by the seniors' lockers. I saw someone who knew me, and once he made the gesture to see if I had smoke, I went to make the sale.

Everything was cool, but not two minutes later, I had an undercover officer hemmin' me up, talkin bout "he saw what I did." Up until then, I knew it was security guards, but I had no clue it was plainclothes police at school, which I guess was the point.

I was searched, cuffed, taken to the police station, and released to staff member from Lawrence Hall on an I-bond. Then I was later told I was being expelled for selling drugs on school property.

The staff member who come and got me was the only one I was really cool with and would talk to. Sammie was twenty-four and came to work there after turning his life around as a teen.

Back on the block

Once out, everything was still poppin'. It'd only been hours, so it wasn't shit to me anyway. In the house, I had proven myself as far as being willing to stand up for myself. In the neighborhood, I still fought almost every time I left the house. The reason being:

1. I was a pretty boy.
2. I wasn't in the local gang.
3. I showed I could get a lil money without them.
4. I wasn't from over there.
5. The girls from over there were showing attention.

Sometimes I won, sometimes I lost, but as long as the boy knew I wasn't scared, I was fine with it.

A few of the girls were cute, but I messed with Jameka the most. She reminded me of Shanquilla in her frame and skin tone. Kendall lived next door, and he liked her too. He'd always pick fights with me, tryin to show out for her.

The craziest thing was that Kendall was cute as fuck to me, and I hated fighting him. I just didn't let him know it. The neighborhood didn't know how I felt about guys. I hid my prissy side well enough. I guess I didn't freak with another boy again until I got put into the Lawrence Hall Alternative School. The juke parties on the block was lit, and I'd get a whole lotta girls dancin' on me, and it felt good, but I ain't fuck them. I was goin to school instead and g'tting' it poppin'.

L.H.A.S

Lawrence Hall Alternative School was located on the Lawrence Hall "Campus" on Lawrence and Francisco. You had the youth agency where the business and therapy was handled, then the school, and then was the group homes that weren't located in other neighborhoods like Avers was.

Here is where I saw the most people showing their rainbow in every capacity, ever more than Northwest Academy. I still felt like a girl in a "boy suit" and didn't know how to embrace myself because of all I'd been taught. Not only was the "no snitching" thing still in, but the whole saying of "No Homo" was heavy in the air in the neighborhood

"No Homo" is a crazy thing to explain. Niggas was real life doing the most gay shit then would say "No Homo" like it made whateva they did not count. This also applied when Lil Wayne and Baby French kicked on 106 Park. It was the same when people said something someone else perceived to be "gay" or "suspect". Anyway, school was where I quietly observed and picked apart everything I was around and dipped a foot in the deep end of the pool of comfortability. It felt good 'cause I hadn't let my hair down in a while.

I learned here these things:

- Straight and not straight people could chill together in a real setting without shit going left. (At the school I was at as a kid, shit was always problematic)
- I liked how well put together Trans females look.
- I was attracted to lesbian "studs" 'cause of the masculine energy.
- I didn't have to act tough all the time.

I sexed and was havin' fun, but at the house, I was still gettin' in trouble for goin' A.W.O.L. Really, we all were, but we ain't care.

Sundays and Such

I started going to church too, but only 'cause it was POPPIN'.

Church in Bolingbrook wasn't like this. On Sundays, you gotta be up and ready. Once you were ready, the van would come around and scoop people from the group homes who wanna go to church. Then, once it was over, we got taken to eat by the agency "Chaplain", who was also the van driver. What I liked most was the ride there, the ride back, and going to eat. Religion wasn't really what I was into.

The fact that other teens from the agency would link up on these Sundays is what had me swingin' through. Jamaica, Keisha, and Eboni were always comin'. They were from the Ewing House and were all Trans teens. "Keisha" turned out to really be Kaylynn. Tekela and Ira's sibling who all of a sudden wasn't around no more at the Hammonds back in the day.

I was most comfortable with Keisha and nem because I could be myself all the way. It takes a lot of energy to "act straight" when you know you not. I would wear myself thin' tryin' to fake it.

In the midst of all this, I turned fifteen, and nigga couldn't tell me shittt!!! I no longer had to fight my way through the neighborhood. My clothes, shoes, hair, and pockets were on point. I did ask Ms. Clark to move me to the Ewing House but she thought I was too "bad" since I was always gettin' into things around the way.

Twan and I were still cool, but I wasn't around him as much. I was around Rio, Bang, Lil Steve, and some more niggas from around the way. We were hitting licks left and right. I got my first gun around this time too. School was still okay; I just had to find a way around the metal detectors.

So now I put a lil more on, bringing the list up to:

- A though demeanor…sometimes.
- The "boy suit" I was living in.
- A sharp tongue verbally.
- The hands to back it up.
- Becoming more of a money–getter.
- A reputation to uphold amongst my lil friends.
- Big dreams and goals.

I guess shit was poppin'. Every blue moon, I thought about life back in Bolingbrook. I missed Keke the most, but I ain't care bout the rest no more. Sammie sometimes used to tell me I should try to communicate. They wanting to talk to me was a thought I didn't really entertain. (I wasn't a compliant kid, but they ain't have to send me away) is what I thought. I felt they ain't want me.

In the hood, I stopped talking to Jameka. I and Jameka's cousin Janise was actin' over bad out there. Janise was too fine, and once we met, it was like somethin' out of a movie the way we'd cut school, link slide, and see what we could get into. She and I was always on each other until around September 17^{th,} 2007.

9-17-07

September this year was the first time I got robbed. School wasn't my thing a lot, so I was hangin' out. Jameka came through with Janise. Janise and I left so we could carry on until late, and Janise wanted me to walk her home. I did, and in the process, I ended up meetin' her whole immediate family, and seein' how much her people loved and cared for her, when we got up to the apartment, it was nice as hell. By the time her people was done grillin' me bout who I was, it was almost midnight.

I slid to the house and stashed my gun by the basement window, then went around to the front to be let in.

After getting let in, I took a shower, changed, and left back out. Coming out the front, Boo man, Kendall, and some other niggas was next door on the stoop. We all was choppin' it up now that Kendall and I wasn't fightin' no more. We parted ways, and I ended up runnin into Teresa's brothers. All I remember was me goin' in the house with some more niggas, and Teresa and I talked a lil. I didn't like her, not like that, but we was cool. Her pops always tried to keep her in the house, but lowkey, niggas was pipin' her down when I was at Roosevelt.

We was smoking, drinkin', and the next thing I knew, I woke up in Swedish Covenant's emergency room, and so fucked up I ain't recognize me. I turned to the side and saw Mr. Robinson, the doctor, and my adopted pops, Mr. Hammond. Once I was clear–headed, Mrs. Robison told me how I got caught slippin' and got left in the front of the group home. No shoes, no money, no jewelry, no phone, and beaten. I asked where my clothes went, and I was told they had to cut em off me since they didn't know where all I was bleeding from.

Shortly after finding out what happened to me, I was whisked away and put back in route to Streamwood. I was real mad because I wanted my "lick back" or revenge. I was told I had to be there for my own safety until Lawrence Hall could figure out what to do with me.

Once there, I was asked the usual questions, and I answered the same as last time.

Only thing I know is that I'm running away to do my things and make money.

****

Two weeks later, to my surprise, I was let go. I just figured it'd be another four months. I remember asking where we were headed to now. I was happy when they said back to Lawrence Hall; now I could do my thing and get back to feeling myself.

Once back in Chicago, I couldn't wait to get out the car, but I was told we were stopping at the Lawrence Hall campus instead of goin back to Avers. That's when I felt somethin' funny was going on.

Turned out I was right to feel funny 'cause after we were at the campus for over an hour, my case worker told me I'd be living at the "Drake" house now, which was on the campus. When I asked about my things, I learned they were already being packed and sent over. They told me I was an at-risk youth and needed more supervision. I wasn't trying to hear it, though. All I knew was I had to get used to a whole new house of people, a whole new neighborhood outside of the campus, and find a whole new way to do what I wanted.

Drake House,
4833 N. Francisco

Drake wasn't bad at all. It had a more structured feel, though, because the staff were a little older. These new dudes I had to be around were iight. It was seven of us, but mostly it was just me, Anthony, and Cory 'cause everyone else was A.W.O.L all the time.

Anthony and lil Cory were too young to be allowed out the door as A.W.O.L. They were only 11. I just wasn't gone 'cause I didn't know the area yet. Outside of school and therapy sessions, the only time I ever was near the campus was when the church van swung through to pick Keisha and them from the Ewing House.

I was assigned a room with Melvin, a 16-year-old boy. Mostly he was gone, but I did recognize him from the church van from time to time. Once he met me as a roommate, we clicked instantly, and before you knew it, we was back A.W.O.L every day.

Being A.W.O.L with Melvin was different than being A.W.O.L when I lived across the bridge on Avers. The area I lived in before was more chill 'cause, although gangs were around, the immediate area was all the same gang. Here, though, I found out we were in the middle of where a few different gangs handled business.

I still wasn't in a gang, but I still had to be on point because, depending on where you were at any time, in someone's hood, things could go down, and just for being there, you could get it too.

After a while, I was into the swing of things. But Melvin got caught with a gun somewhere and went to jail. During this time, I stuck around the house more and leaned into music and art. Even as a kid, I liked to draw, write raps, and listen to music. This is how me and Tony Evans got cool. Tony Evans worked at Drake House but also was into art and music. After learning more about him, I learned and liked the fact that he was local DJ on the side.

For a while, he and I would focus on me honing my crafts, and I liked it, but the deal was he'd only fuck with me if I stopped running away.

The more I stayed around, the better I got at drawing and rapping. However, I was missing how shit was back up on Avers. Rapping and drawing was cool, but it wasn't paying off 'cause I never did anything with the songs I recorded. Looking back, I wish I had focused on myself instead of giving in to the call of the street. Maybe I could have ended up with a record deal.

Living on campus put me closer to Keisha and them, and it was fine with me. By now, I considered myself to be bisexual, but I still couldn't tell anybody. I thought nobody would understand, so I kept it to myself. As far as the things I did with the people I did them with, it ain't go on farther than that.

I did end up linking back up with Janise. I never got tired of her, but it was not just her. Now it was Anita and Gabby too. I met Anita through a DCFS event and Gabby through Melvin one day we were out and about. I liked all three, but it ain't keep me away from swinging through church on Sunday.

It's crazy how thinly I spread myself between everything I had going on, but that's just how things had to be. This "boy suit" was getting stuffy, though. A bitch was dying to breathe! Imagine being how I was a child, "changing" to blend in on the outside, but still feeling like a girl on the inside. On top of that, being physically small and having to go overboard to get my point across so people wouldn't run over me. I also had to go hard in the streets so people would know I could go even harder, even though I was a pretty boy. Being a pretty boy was the only way I could indulge in shoes, clothes, jewelry, and hairstyles without being clocked as feminine by the guys.

The only times I came close to "slipping" was when I'd be at the store, looking at all the bras, panties, jewelry, clothes, and makeup. When I'd be shopping, I'd get caught up in my own lil world as I imagined being all prettied up. But I couldn't look for too long, so I kept movin'.

2008-Summer

It wasn't long before Lawrence Hall was tired of me. I did too much, and they no longer wanted the stress of being responsible. Two months after I turned sixteen, I was packed up and sent out of Chicago to the Allendale Association in Lake Villa.

Allendale

Allendale was in Lake Villa, Illinois. This was the farthest shit I'd ever been to at the time. It seemed like the middle of nowhere. That wasn't shit, though, 'cause once I got there, my file did too, and they decided to put me in the Benet Lake boys' home, which was all boys and off campus.

I knew I fucked up by the time I got there. Allendale seemed to be in the middle of nowhere and Benet Lake was even more remote, surrounded by cornfields and all that! I learned that this was where the boys who liked to run away were sent.

Imagine my face when I realized I was in Bristol, Wisconsin. I knew the trip from Chicago seemed long, but it must've been the stop in Lake Villa that tricked me into thinkin it wasn't that long. I was sick to my stomach immediately, but this was my life now, and I had to get used to it.

Benet Lake "The Box"

First and foremost, once I got there, I didn't leave my room for two days. I was in a slump and didn't want to be there. I couldn't go anywhere, though, 'cause from what I saw upon arrival, there was nowhere to go.

Once I got hungry, I had to come out and be around the boys. In the cafeteria, I ate a little and sat alone. I felt naked 'cause the boys were all coming and just sizing me up. It was at least twenty of us total, minus the staff.

After eating, I decided to explore the place a little since id have to be there.

There was so many rooms with two boys in each room, a cafeteria, a "day room" with a TV and seats, a "rec room" with workout equipment, a PlayStation, and a pool table, a laundry room, a school wing, and outside was a basketball hoop surrounded by...you guessed it, a whole lot of nothing.

In the room, there were two beds, a bathroom with a sink, toilet, a stand-up shower, and a window.

As soon as I saw the window, I was happy because I knew if I ever wanted to leave, that's how I'd bounce. My happiness died immediately when I learned the window open fully but set off an alarm after the first three inches were opened.

Broken

I was smaller than all the boys, and it was obvious to me that my throw off weren't working. I didn't play sports, didn't watch sports, and didn't do anything to mess up my hair, clothes, or shoes ever. There were no girls to distract them, so when the boys watched me, they figured me out quickly. At first, I was okay, but it took less than two weeks for me to get messed with sexually. I didn't want it, and he was too big to fight and win. One day, I went into the rec room, finding myself alone. Tony Brown came in, cut the lights out, and sat next to me on the couch by the PlayStation. I didn't think anything at first, I thought he wanted to play Madden with me. However, it wasn't long before he was all up on me into my ear, tellin me that he knows wassup with me. He put his hands down my shorts and kept me pinned in place. I tried to stop him, but he was too strong. The more I moved, the more aggressive he got, and I froze up 'cause I got scared. To this day, I remember how it felt as he manhandled me, got my clothes off and had his way with me, while threating to hurt me if I told. I remember how it felt to put my clothes on and go in my room, shower, and the sting of the water as it reached where I was violated. I was different when I came out my room after that incident. I lashed out at anyone who came too close, and fought with anyone who said anything too crazy.

The worst part was seeing how Tony Brown looked at me, knowing that he took a piece of me. Tony Brown turned 18 and aged out of being there shortly after the incident. Until now, I've never mentioned what he did to me to anybody ever. This event was now basically 13 years ago.

Trouble

Anyway, I quickly learned what happened when you got in trouble here. It wasn't just no write-up here; it meant lockdowns, and the staff enforced it. No outings, no rec room, no going to shoot hoops, no day room, no nothing. On top of it, I disliked the staff 'cause the majority of them would overdo it when it came to breaking up a fight or handling you when you was wildin'. One minute you gettin' it in, and the next minute all you know is these big ass niggas put you on ya shit and bendin' you up at impossible angles, talkin' bout calm down or it'll be worse.

Searches Roy

We also had to comply with pat-down searches every time we left or came back to make sure we had no cell phones, money, weapons, or drugs. By the time I experienced the searches, everybody felt I was different, but I just wouldn't say it. I was scared to open up. One of the staff, named Roy, used to take this to his advantage. I used to hate when he searched me 'cause he always took extra feels on my thighs and ass. It was so creepy the way he'd mumble under his breath as he'd do it. I used to love his days off 'cause I knew I wouldn't be felt the way he would. I was bone-skinny, small, short, with long hair, and was quietly prissy, but I was tired of people doing things to me.

Protected

Time went on, and on my first trip to Walmart with the other boys, I slid to the section where all the outdoors shit was. I had to make it quick, and since I knew the layout of pretty much any Walmart, I was able to sneak a knife, open it up, hide it, and make it back to the group before it seemed like I was up to anything. I didn't want to be mistaken for A.W.O.L!

I didn't really talk much at first, and even after being there for a while, I didn't know who to trust, to be honest.

I loved stuffed animals and had a couple in my room. So after stealing the knife, and getting' it back in and hiding the knife from the search that day, I cut open the stuffed dog and hid the knife inside. I kept it close and wasn't found out because the dog came with a little sweater, and I cut where the sweater concealed the stuffing.

Now that I felt secure and protected, I had to figure out how to get some money. This clearly wasn't Chicago, and things were way different here. Most the boys were bad, but they didn't seem to have been through what I had or lived how I did before I got there. So much as I didn't want to, I had to put myself around them more if I wanted to figure out what my next move would be.

Fair Exchange

With these boys, videos games and electronics in general were the best things smoking. By now, I'd had a couple of visits with the Hammonds, but after coming up, being sent away, and goin' through the life I'd lived up to now, I didn't feel like I fit. So when times would come where the other boys would go and see their families, I'd stay back, go out to stores, steal games and small electronics, and when the boys got back, they'd give me money their family gave them in exchange for whatever items I had.

Now that I had a way to keep money again, I couldn't stop. I had to have it, and nothing was worse to me than to want something and not being able to have it in a store. I knew I didn't have enough to run away like I'd want, but I had enough to make being at "The Box" a little easier for me.

It wasn't long after I started gettin' money that the staff started to take notice. I was now wearing things they didn't provide, poppin' up with jewelry, havin' a few different electronics I couldn't explain, and most of the boys fucked with me 'cause they liked what I provided.

One day a younger staff member came into my room and asked me how I made money. I played dumb even though we were cool. I didn't know if the other staff had sent him. He asked me if I was into prescription pills. I wasn't. He asked me if I knew if the other boys would want any. I told him I didn't know. But once he told me he had some, if I found someone, I knew he wasn't gonna tell about me havin' money. So we got even cooler, and I'd only go to places if he was taking us, so that I could really do what I needed. In exchange, I wouldn't mention shit and would lie about where this staff took me when asked.

Step Down

Life was this way all the way until September 2009. I did a good job stayin' out of the way, so the staff figured it was time to step me down to somewhere less restrictive. They asked where I wanted to go. I told them back to Chicago, But they told me that shit was NOOOT happening. After giving a couple options a look, I was placed at the Larkin Center in Elgin.

Being away from "the box" was the best feeling. My only focus now was how I can make a whole lot of money. I had $1,104 to my name. I was now seventeen and knew nobody in this new place. Things would change, though.

College St.

College Street was crazy to me. Here I am, fresh in the house, wary that shit could go left, and only to find out I was the oldest one in the house. School let out for them, and once I met everyone, I'm left like, "The fuck I'm doin' with these lil niggas?"

Settling in wasn't bad, though. I learned how the staff move and the layout of the house. Here it was only myself and five boys. Five boys who, after meeting me, decided to watch my every move.

Because of all I'd done and been through up to now, I developed an exterior so tough and thuggy that one would never believe I'd been so feminine before it. The only thing is I still ain't know how to really show these boys how to become young men in a way society could accept. I couldn't, well, wouldn't acknowledge my femininity in a heathy way. So what I ended up doin' was overthuggin', and that's all the boys knew from me.

Well, school time came for me again, but I wasn't feelin it. Big surprise, or nah? What I was surprised about was where I ended up going. There were three options: the Larkin Center's alternative school, Gifford, an unrelated alternative school, and the regular high school.

I'm like 'send me to the regular school'. They said they thought Gifford would be a better option, which was crazy to me 'cause this was supposed to be a fresh slate of sorts.

Gifford's turned out to be the most chill alternative school I'd ever been to. The only thing that was dumb to me was that we had to wear uniforms, a royal blue polo collar shirt and khaki pants, the Jake from State Farm type outfit. The school was co-ed, and it felt good to be around girls. I hadn't had much interaction with any since Chicago. I mean, meeting them on outings at Benet Lake or, let's saaayy, Target, DID NOT count.

A few days went by as a new student, and at lunch is where it happened. I met Brooklyn.

Hello Brooklyn

Light skin, my height, pretty hair, cute face, slight frame. Time seemed to slow down when I met her. Most of all, I liked how she told shit how it was and seemed real carefree. I still felt exactly about myself how I feel to this day, but Brooklyn turned me ON.

The more time I spent with her, the less time I was on College St. I was with her at her Auntie's house on St. Charles St. Being on St. Charles was exactly what I needed. Brooklyn's Auntie Pebbles really was just a female version of the older guys I used to know in Chicago. Once she learned where I lived, she told me I was always welcome.

Over there, it was Brooklyn, me, Hag, Cartwright, J.B most the time. Hag and Cartwright was Pebble's kids, well, the last two who lived there. J.B was Pebble's sister Sheila's son. They all fucked with me hard and didn't treat me funny based on where I came from.

Brooklyn and I as a couple was cool at first. It just sucked whenever the police would stop us and then do me for being A.W.O.L. 'Cause then I'd have to leave the group home and walk alll the way back over again. Sexually, shit was poppin' too. Brooklyn seemed to keep up with me in every way.

Hag, well, Shakeisha was pretty as fuck, though she was usually in her room or with her kids and her baby daddy. Cartwright was iight. He was always into something. But J.B and I was ova cool. He always made sure I was iight and acted like my older brother wherever we went.

All this took place over the course of a month. I wasn't coming to school for classes, really. After a lil while, Brooklyn and I would bounce. I was fine with that 'cause I didn't know much of the schoolwork. One day I ended up getting suspended, and that would end up being the start of it all going left. This is what happened.

What Happened

The group home did room searches. I kept my shit together, but I kept weapons and shit at school in my locker because I was told if my room was searched and anything illegal was found, they'd call the police. I got suspended, and I went to school just so J.B and I could drop Brooklyn off. She asked me to run to the store for her so she could get to class on time. I did. I smoked on the way back. I came in the side door, dropped off Brooklyn her shit, and on the way out, I was stopped by security. I smelled like weed, so they searched me. I wasn't supposed to even be there, so I tried to leave. I was escorted to the office where I was questioned. I cussed them and the principal out and sat around a while.

I didn't know that while I was in the office, my locker was being searched. My face dropped when weapons were brought in along with my school I.D. Here I was, high blown, in trouble, and about to go to jail. I was the saltiest bitch alive when the cuffs clamped on me. With all the odd shit happening at schools, sayin', "It ain't what it looks like" wasn't gonna work.

It Still Ain't What
It Looked Like

At the station, I was gettin' drilled on why I had weapons on school grounds. They asked, "Who you wanna hurt? Are you plotting against someone who suspended you?" I was like, "Naw, I ain't into that type of shit," and then proceeded to explain how I'd been through a few things, was new around there, just felt more comfortable with weapons because of my size, and only had them in my locker so didn't risk getting caught in a room search at home. Then they asked why I was at school while being suspended, saying I was trespassing, and I'm sittin' there like, "I just ran to the store for my girl and brought her her shit." Ain't work! And I was off to the station.

After what seemed like forever, I was booked in for having weapons on school property and for storing in my locker. It sucked but was better than the whole "You probably was gonna use 'em on someone" type shit they was tryin' to lay on me at first. Next, I was shuffled into a paddy wagon and taken to the county jail, all while trying to wrap my mind around the charges of unlawful possession and storage of weapons. Really like, what was about to become of it. After a bumpy and uncomfortable ride, I found out quick.

Kane County Jail

First off, I was scared. But I wasn't gonna show it. I thought I might go to Juvie, but nope! Since I was seventeen, they charged me as an adult, and there I went. The first thing I remember about this place, aside from being scared, was how much it stank. It was sooo stinky in there, but everyone else seemed like they ain't notice. After being processed and enduring a few jokes from the guards about how small I was, I was taken to an 8-person cell. I later learned it was the part of the jail where petty crimes and non-violent first-timers go. But for me, it might as well been Alcatraz, given how shook I was about it.

I literally was sick to my stomach most the time I was there. It seemed forever, and I missed Brooklyn and everybody. I didn't know what was goin' to happen on a day-to-day basis, never mind the long run.

At court, I got a bond of $17.000. It wasn't a lot of money, but it might as well have been a million 'cause I couldn't pay it, Brooklyn couldn't pay it, and Pebbles ain't have it either. 10% percent of $17,000 was all that separated me from getting out. I told my public defender (state-appointed lawyer) how badly I wanted to go home, how

Christmas was coming, and blah, blah, blah. It hadn't been long, but I was ready to go.

Meanwhile, as I waited for my court date to come around, I met Aja. Aja was in the same cell block while I was downstairs. Aja stood tall with light skin and long hair, and I couldn't look away. Aja was in for retail theft and was only doin' "county time". This wasn't the first time I'd been around a transgender person, but this was just the first time I'd been around someone like this beside me in a while. Although I guess I ain't count 'cause I kept my prissy on the inside….smh.

Anyway, we got cool and learned about each other. The craziest thing at the time was finding out Aja and Pebbles was cousins, and she knew Brooklyn. The next crazy shit was how Aja saw through my exterior like an X-ray and tapped at the girl I was tryin' to hide. It was scary when she told me what she sensed about me. It's funny, though, 'cause now I can sense shit in certain niggas who be around me where I live now, even when they act tough.

Let's Makes a Deal

Anyway, November rolled around, and it was time for court again. I still wanted to make it home for Christmas next month. Aja and I met our "P.D.s" in the side rooms before heading into separate courtrooms. My P.D., as public defenders were known, had a big smile on his face and told me he got an offer on a table. The offer was, "Sign here, and you'll be out in about a week. You'll have an ankle monitor for a lil while, and you'll only be on probation for two years."

All I cared about was "Sign here, and you'll be out," so I signed my life away and got the fuck out. Lookin' back, I woulda just stayed in the county.

The ankle bracelet wasn't shit. I just wanted to see Brooklyn. But picture my face when, on the way home from the county, I stopped at the corner store to use they phone and turned to the right, only to see Brooklyn and some nigga all hugged up in there. I coulda acted a whole ass, but there wasn't any point. What could she say? Tell me it ain't what it looked like?

Aftermath

I made it home, took a shower, and contacted the ankle bracelet people. I guess this bracelet was to make sure I didn't run away before I saw my probation officer.

I met my probation officer at her office on Grove St.

Rachel Buchman wasn't for none. Once the ankle bracelet came off, she made it clear I wasn't off the hook. No running away, no skipping school, and no drugs. I left her office and was like, "Yeah, iight."

I got registered back at Streamwood, not the behavior center but the alternative school where I lost my virginity way back when Northwest Academy in Streamwood hadn't changed much, except I was the older student now. I went for a couple of weeks and bounced. Shit wasn't for me.

The group home staff found out I wasn't goin' to school and was like, "You don't gotta go to school, you don't have to work a job, but you can be here all day." So, I left. Every day "A.W.O.L" was nothing. But it was crazy walking around and going places Brooklyn and I used to go alone. One day, I was at the house and ran across Aja's information. I'd put all the paperwork from jail on my shelf and forgot about it. I came out of my room and asked one of the staff where Park St. was. She looked at me crazy and was like, "You be leavin' every day and don't know where it is?" I was like, "nah." Sharon looked at me and was like, "boy, it's the next block over." I was like, "cool," and I left.

411 Park-Pullin' at My Put-Ons

I was in my feelings about Brooklyn, so I wasn't checkin' for nobody. But once I met with Aja outside of jail, I was told I'd be okay.

Every time I went over, I'd learn or see somethin' from Aja. I studied her the way I used to study Keke, Mama, Aunt Mag, and everybody when I was young.

She taught me everything she knew and introduced me to "The Family".

One night, she sat me down and was like, "So, you a boy or a girl?" My heart sped up cause I knew what she meant, but with all I'd put "on", it was hard to say out loud. So she asked questions, and I and answered till she and I got to the bottom of it.

Aja stayed in a studio apartment and didn't have much, but I was welcome to anything and to stay there if I wanted.

Staying over there was hard 'cause I still was on probation. It felt good to be welcome, but I was nervous whenever I had to go to see my P.D. I wasn't doin' anything big, but I wasn't following my probation stipulations. Ms. Buchman told me to see about a job then.

Job hunting was rough. I was 17, now a felon with no job experience anywhere. Nobody would take a chance on me, from Burger King to the funeral homes I got "no's" I was tired of being boxed in, wanted to break free from living like this.

New Job

One day, I was at Aja's spot, and this light-skinned, thick, Stacey dash–lookin' bitch came through. I learned her name and listened as she was talkin' bout how this guy was hung too big for her, but she took it like 6 'cause she was gettin paid. Tory was soo fine, and I knew she could help me cause she looked as paid as she said she was. However, I got shy and found out everything I needed to know from Aja after Tory left.

Tory was Aja's cousin and was related to Pebbles and them too. I was completely shocked when I learned how easy I could get in on the money.

Sex for money was the best thing to me. I liked sex and money. What I didn't always like was who wanted some of me, but it wasn't about likes. I was still playin' pretty boy but was goin' for guys and females. I didn't care, though. By now, I had become really good at sex period, which came in handy 'cause a session is set up for a certain period of time, and if your date cum before the session's time expires, the session ends anyway. So the quicker you come, the faster I could shower, smoke, and move to the next person who tryin' to see me.

Prostituting didn't make me feel a way at all, though. I went to havin' things that I didn't have before. Well, not since before I moved out to here.

A funny thing happened at the house, though. The young boys all loved when I'd come through, but the staff was on my ass heavy. One staff member took a likening to me in more than a "platonic" way. I was 17, she was 36, but told me she was 28. She would link with me on the low when we was at the house, and she'd pull up on me when her shift ended at the house. Her name was Angel

Being older, she dropped all kinda jewels on me mentally, but I wasn't tryin' to take it further than us talkin' and fuckin'. When she took me out to her home I knew shit was going to get heavy, but I really ended up liking her. When she told me I could stay there, I was conflicted, torn between living with her and living my life back at Aja's. I ended up easing up off angel, and doing my shit on Park St.

March 2010

Time went on, and it was March 2010. I'd just seen my P.O and told her I was doing odd jobs. I was heading up College Street when I turned around. I saw a woman with chocolate skin, a model's walk, slim with slight curves. I wanted to talk, but I got shy and kept walking. I went past the group home and was almost to the end of the block when I turned around again. I threw the shy shit aside and let her catch up to me before I spoke up close. She put me in the mind of "New York" from TV shows on VH1, and when I heard her speak, that was all it took. I got her number, and Jayda and I made plans to meet later.

I went to Aja's, smoked, and hung out with her. She told everybody she was like my mama 'cause she took me in. Everybody was comin' over, so I kicked it with them then left to see Jayda.

Jayda was even finer the second time I saw her. We walked, talked, kicked it, smoked, and then she took me to where she lived. The area across town was much quieter and nicer than what I knew about.

Once at her spot, we was bout to get it poppin', and Jayda was like, "Hold up, lemme tell you something." I looked at her in her eyes and was like, "What?" She told me she was a "T girl" and asked if it was a problem. I laughed and told her she pretty and all, but I knew already. Growing up how I grew up, you figured shit out like this quickly. We laughed for a while, and then she gave me some top. Before I dipped, I sucked her soul out too.

What did but shouldn't have surprised me, was when I took Jayda to meet Aja, they already knew each other. In OUR community, everybody knows everybody, and most of us were in the same line of work. I would pop in and out of the group home to talk shit to the staff and the other kids, but to be honest, I didn't really need the Larkin Center no more. I felt I found my crowd elsewhere. I did link with Angel still from time to time.

Heating Up April

I turned eighteen and spent it with Jayda. She cooked, smoked, drank, and everything. I was touched 'cause it was a nice night for me that I didn't expect. We spent almost every night and day together, whether we was at her house or she was at Park St. with me and Aja. I rarely took the time to slow down, which was my downfall sometimes.

****

Elgin being small as it is, was still really a place where you could slide and be private, but in the long run, you never knew when you'd cross paths with someone you didn't expect to see.

I was out and about one day when I saw J.B and some of his friends. I hadn't seen him since he and Brooklyn would come to my court dates after the school thing.

He asked me how come I ain't come around no more and how I was making money. I explained what I saw with Brooklyn when I got out, and he was like, "Mannn, fuck that, come thru." So I started coming around again.

Now let's check the put-ons:

- I'm 18, feelin' pretty grown…smh…ain't know shit really.
- Getting money by prostitution/fuckin' any gender for play and pay.
- Feeling comfortable only around my crowd.
- Turn my "girl" off when I'm around straight people. :-(
- Not outwardly tough actin', more of a "show you when it gets there" type.
- Still had goals.
- Didn't use feelings much to protect myself.
- Playin' innocent at P.O so I could stay out. Fuck violating probation.

Getting hotter May 2010

In the midst of all this, I slide to the group home one day, on some high shit. I sat on the stoop, and Angel came out. We talked our shit, but then she got serious and told me my stuff not there. How the agency thought it'd be better for me to live at the house with older boys across town, and how the younger boys were starting to try to follow my lead. The last part felt weirdest 'cause I ain't make myself out to be a role mode. I parted ways, and went across town to see wassup at this other home.

510 Highland, all the way out there.

I got there, and for a minute, it felt like I was at a grown version of "Avers" back in Chicago. All the staff were 8, 10, or more years older than us. I can't even name more than two boys who lived here 'cause EVERYBODY was A.W.O.L from the moment I got there. I never even met the guy who I was paired up in the room with. I didn't care, though, 'cause even though I was now across town from Aja, J.B, and everybody, I was only 10 minutes from Jayda.

Probation wasn't going good either. I was fuckin' up. No school, always A.W.O.L, couldn't explain my job in a believable way, and I dropped dirty for weed for the third time in a row.

Once I pissed in that cup, I knew it was over, so I didn't stick around in case she decided to take me in for violating terms. As I left, I was told to "look for my court summons in the mail". Damn. "Now I'm probably going back to jail," is what I thought. Violate probation enough, and you go to court. Your probation gets terminated, and the initial charges you got on probation to get brought back up, and you get more probation or time. I just didn't know it.

****

Between Aja, making money, fucking police, Jayda, Angel, and coming around J.B and them, it was a lot. J.B was trappin' and wanted to know how I was gettin' my money. Brooklyn and I was kickin it sometimes, but I was doin' me, and it looked like she was on the same shit, turnin' up but not gettin' no money. I wanted to show her how to get paid off her coochie, but decided against it. Speaking of gettin' paid, I ran into Tory at a party in the Mills. We dipped, and I was surprised to find out she got a dick. I've known people before and after her, but she was seamless and put together in a way that made her tea damn near impossible to clock. We don't talk now, but she still holds the title of one of the prettiest transwomen I ever played with.

****

Anyway, I ended up meeting my nigga outside after coming from seeing a friend of mine. He was all over my friend when we walked up, but got off her 'cause she a girl. She just was real boyish and ain't look like a girl. Once he got on me, we exchanged numbers, and me and my friend left.

Flemmy wasn't my guy at first, though. We kicked it, he wanted to fuck. I told him what I cost, and he paid. We hung like that for a while. But one night, we were in the Coloniel, a fucked af motel on Villa St. and he stuck around after we got done doin' business. He asked how many people I've let sex me for money. I told him the truth that I don't keep up with it. He then told me and showed me how he got plenty of money. He dressed, drove, and talked in a way that made me think he sold drugs. However, I found out I was only half right.

The play Flemmy put down is, he robs, then buys drugs to sell, sells them, thus making a profit. He and his brother were both part of this operation.

I was in, but he wanted to keep me for himself sexually. The way I saw it, I wasn't feeling the whole "leave everything alone and fuck with me" aspect. Mainly because if you do that, and shit go left, you gotta start all over. So, I juggled everything and everybody while still holding onto my past and put-ons.

****

Reality hit me when it was time for court. I'd been doing everything under the sun and didn't want to go, but Jayda made me. So I went, and for violating was told I'd to serve

90 days. I told the judge okay but asked for a few days to get my affairs in order. He did me even better and granted me two weeks before I'd have to turn myself in warning that I "wouldn't like what would happen if I blew court".

I stepped out the courthouse feeling like I dodged a bullet, but I was hit with one when I saw Angel a couple days later.

500 Degrees

Angel told me she was pregnant, and it was only me who was fuckin'. I was too through 'cause not only did I have a lot goin' on, and now a baby. She was way convincing, so when we parted ways I turned up everything I was doing to be able to try to afford raising a baby.

As if this wasn't enough, Brooklyn turned up pregnant, and her pops got on me at a cookout a few days after that.

I was fuckin', robbin', trappin' way hard, and the court was out the picture. I blew that shit and was now on the run. I had to be careful 'cause the police knew me off countless missing person reports, run-ins, running from the drug unit, and that school shit from 2009. I wasn't trying to get caught. Especially not with drugs and my gun, a 17-shot 9mm.

The more time I spent with Flemmy, the less time I could spend around everyone else. But for now, it had to be this way. Having Flemmy with me, everything felt fine, the only thing about him that blew me was his jealousy. Every time I wasn't around him and came back around, I had to go through the third degree about where I was, who I was with, and what I was doin'. I liked him, so I ended up not going away from him much to keep the arguments down.

****

His brothers and sisters all knew I was different from the moment they met me, but everything was cool. None of 'em acted funny.

I learned even more places around town through Flemmy, but my favorite was the Trap, owned by one of Flemmy's homies. The first time I went in, I fell in love. EVERYTHING was goin' on you could think of. I was there day and night, and sometimes I'd see some of the boys who was supposed to be at the group home on Highland.

At this point, I was wilding and felt like shit would never end. But it did.

7-20-10

One night, I was at the Trap after making a pickup with Flemmy. I'd hit a lick a few nights before, and barely made it out. Midway through me baggin' up my work, I got thirsty. I told Flemmy I was headed to the store for two-liter of pineapple crush. When I walked out the house, I felt fine.

I preferred to walk at night because if anything happened, I had a better chance of getting away than having to drive. Anyway, I made it to the store, and headed back when my stomach started turning. I kept walking but was on alert 'cause my gut don't lie.

I couldn't put my finger on what was wrong, but I started thinking that someone could be out to get me. I've been caught before, but I've gotten down on people too.

As I made it right past the group home, I started hearing gravel crunching. Someone was behind me. I didn't wanna look, but I needed to know what I was dealing with. I faked a sneeze and looked back. It was Detective Jensen and his boys, creeping in one of the many undercover cars they had access to.

I couldn't believe they got up on me like this, but I did know if I was going to jail, they would have to work for it.

I made it to the end of the block, cut right, and took off. I'd outran Jensen plenty of times before, so it wasn't shit.

What I didn't know was that they were prepared this time. The chase lasted a while, and then I got under a truck, I thought it was over as I watched them go back and forth. However, I was wrong. When I saw the K-9 unit pull up, I took back off 'cause I wasn't beating no dog in running. I needed to get as far as I could before they let the dog loose. I ran and ran. But it was clear that they wanted me by how many different cars started cutting me off.

Once I got up Washington Street, I had hope. The Trap was just a block up. I got closer when Jensen and them turned up the street. I felt sick 'cause I knew I couldn't run into the Trap now. They would kick the door in to get me and find all type of shit, plus some of the other people who were on they're radar. I couldn't be the cause of a whole house goin' down, so I kept on running past the Trap.

In a last ditch effort, I hopped some fences to get through backyards hoping to throw them off. I got in somebody's backyard, but couldn't get over the fence for shit. My height wouldn't let it happen. However, I kept tryin' till the backyard flooded with police and I was tackled to the ground and handcuffed at gunpoint. Damn…

All Over

I was taken in, booked, interrogated, and left for two days before I was rebooked for additional charges. I was then shuffled into a van, headed to the county.

Going to the county again wasn't shit 'cause I knew what to expect as for as processing. What I didn't know was when I'd ever be free again. I was replaying my life in my head, and could only hope for a sentence that would let me still be young when I got out.

****

I was the saltiest when court came around, and I was taken back in front of the judge I skipped court on. He made good on his promise, though. Two months later, I had 5 years for that school shit, and 12 years for the armed robbery I got booked for. I had to serve 50% of my time before I'd be free again. I was only lucky that both sentences were run together. Leaving the county on the way to prison, I couldn't help but wonder what would happen between now and then.

Statesville NRC and Beyond

This is the first stop when sentenced to do real time. This is where you are stripped, evaluated, and stored until they figure out which prison to send you to. It stank, had roaches, rats, mold, and all kinds shit, I was SCARED_TO_DEATH but couldn't act like it. I was roomed with an old man for eight days before I was put on a bus headed to the Lincoln parking lot, which was the "transfer pad". This was where all different buses from different prisons met to swap us out. I found out where I was headed wasn't so bad. They told me I'd be okay there.

Part: 2

Dixon

Dixon C.C. was not bad at all. It's got three separate levels of prisons, located throughout. I was set as a low medium. Here I was 5'5" and around 130ish pounds, soaking wet, tryin' to seem hard around the block…umm no! I had to have serval seats. I wasn't fooling ANYBODY, even after Flemmy told my naive ass to "play straight" and say you part of this gang. OMG that shit was a super fail, and before you know it, I was suckin' and fuckin' all around that place. It's crazy how life works where the more you try to hide a part of you, the more you find yourself in situations where it's impossible to hide in.

My cellmate, Polo, was who called me out on my Femininity. He then spilled his own tea with me one night. He was 19, I was 18, and we were cool. Anyway, once he called me out, I couldn't hide, and the "boy suit" was getting too small to wear. So, once I came clean, and he spoke his part, we started fuckin' around with each other.

****

Once people started catching on to us, it got crazy. One night, I was up with Polo, and I was on his lap. Next thing you know, a trustee named Nuki came down the hall sweeping. Then he came by the door, and I glanced up. We caught eye contact. Next thing I know, the following morning, it seemed like everybody was watching Polo and I up and down the block. I heard the comments as we passed people in the halls.

We ain't care, though, I was iight, and so was he. But we came to a head when we went to the hole after one of the guards caught him beating me up one night during a disagreement. It was written up as a fight, but everybody knows that if you get a ticket for fighting, you should deny it or try to talk it down to a horse-playing ticket in front of the adjustment committee. They're the ones who hear tickets, expunge 'em, or sole out consequences, which usually involve a loss of some type of privileges, hole time, revocation of good time, or whatever. Anyway, we were out the hole after 14 days, so we ain't care.

The funny thing is, the rumor mills in prison are worse than the high school ones. So once out the hole, I heard that everybody said Polo and I got put in the hole for getting caught fucking! I was tooo thru, but that wasn't all. Now, the gang dudes were on my ass for makin' 'em "look bad", and "The Community" were side–eyein' the fuck out me like, "Oh, you runnin' with them, but you really one of us".

So then, as time went on, I started shedding the put-ons and really hung out with people who were in the LGBTQ+ community, whether they were out and proud, or like me, who was steady dipping a toe out the prison closet, as Flemmy said I'd be safe in.

Over the course of a year and some change, I was clearly "out", but I couldn't stay out of trouble. I was steadily getting wrote up for being in someone's room or having someone in my room. I didn't feel the sting of the write–ups, though. Then everything fell apart. Flemmy got locked up, my money ran out, and I was on the guards' radar 'cause of how I was getting wrote up. It was hard for a while, but then one of the guys put an older guy on me. He was basically thirty years my senior. His name was Johnathan. He had a healthy account and bought me anything I wanted, as long as I let him fuck whenever, wherever, and kept his dick sucked and his toes curling.

Johnathan was iight at first. He was cute, but the money was cuter. He was in a gang too and was one of the ones who had "clout". So nobody acted funny to him, not even when I got caught suckin' his dick by some younger guys who was in the same gang as him.

Once that happened, though, all the down-low dudes were tryin' to see me. That's when I found out that Johnathan not only was jealous AF, but he also came to the conclusion he owned me 'cause he took care of me. The jealousy and rage he'd show turned him from cute to ugly in my eyes, and I wasn't feelin' him no more.

Like a dumb hoe, though, I stayed with him to do what he wanted 'cause I needed money, and he had it. This went on until the day after I turned twenty. We were taken to the hole after a guard bussed the cell down and caught me on my knees, mid suck, with a throatful of dick. What happened next played out like a blur, but yup, I was in handcuffs quicker than you could say, "It's not what it looks like!"

In the following week, I was found guilty on my write-up and was told that the adjustment committee was done seein' me around since I clearly didn't care about the rules. I got two months hole time and a disciplinary transfer to a "more secure" facility.

I should've known shit could get real, but I didn't have another prison to compare at the time. The part that did me in was when I found myself shackled on the transfer bus, being asked if I could fight after I told the guy next to me the name of where I was slated to go.

Shawnee C.C

The bus ride to Shawnee was the longest ride I've been on ever. Back then, to now, nine years later, no ride has beaten that one. Turns out, Shawnee is at the southernmost border of Illinois. Shit, one good spit and it lands in Kentucky. I didn't see much that one day, though. I went there as a punishment. So as soon as I was off the bus, to the hole I went to finish the last lil hole time a couple days after I was released from the hole into the general population. I was fucked up instantly at the sight of all the barbed wire, all the hopeless looks on the faces of the guys I walked past, and how the buildings here were what later was explained to me as X-Houses due to their shape.

Once on deck, shit… it was of control. People were literally doing whatever they wanted, and it was no cameras back then. Oh yea, this was also one of the youngest wings where none of us were over 25. Off the rip, it was clear to my eyes that bitches like me weren't welcome. So before I even uttered a word, I put my girl away and decided that stuffy ass boy suit was what was going to get me through around here. I put back on all the put-ons I could and bopped around the thuggiest way imaginable. It worked for a while till it didn't.

See, sometimes my mannerisms would give me away, and then nigga would be lookin' upside my shit like I was in a silent round in the hot seat. I could talk the most shit and pop the flyest gang shit ever, but it wasn't enough. I was still too pretty for niggas liking, and niggas got to whispering and dropping hints left and right that they felt I was sweet. This happened every time I ever landed anywhere new in life up to this point, so I should've been ready. But once again, I felt naked AF in the eyes of my peers. Being "me" wasn't safe, though, so I played the comments and stares off until I was pushed across the line that separated "feeling naked" and "being naked".

Down there, you were in the cell for 21, maybe 22 hours a day, and it was set up where the gangs was doin' the most, and anything could happen. Everybody was watching everybody. One day, though, I called myself being slick. Since my cellmate had school in the mornings, that's when I would get some. But since I had nobody to give me dick, I got mine by gettin' it poppin with a soap dick. Yes, I said soap dick, but it's better than it sounds. You take soap (a lot of it), bust it down, wet it up, sculpt it, let it dry, wrap it up, and you good to go. The only thing is, you gotta get rid of it A.S.A.P 'cause you didn't wanna risk getting it found during a cell search. You can't get a ticket for it, but it'd probably embarrass you to death if whoever found it got announcing it and waving it around upon its discovery. (Back then I would've fell out! Now, I wouldn't give a fraction of a fuck).

Anyway, my cellmate was at school, and I was hot! He'd be gone a couple hours, so I did my thing. So much so that I didn't realize he was back on the block till it was too late. I was in the middle of the floor, naked, poppin my coochie as I rode the fuck out my toy which was in me to the hilt, and propped on my small property box. All I heard was the "click, whoosh" sound off the door lock and the door being opened. I heard "What the Fuck?!" as I spun around, still on the dick, and caught eye contact with my cellmate. It was the longest three second of my life. He saw me, as I saw him seeing me, as he all but fainted!!

He ain't know how to handle what he saw. Soon as I opened my mouth to say something, he just eased the door closed, as if nothing went down. I wondered where he was going.

Now look, I don't know where he went, to this day. But when he came back in the room, it was clear he ain't know what to do with himself. A couple days later, he got himself moved, and I was in the room alone till I got sent to another wing where someone else just lost a cellmate.

Y'all know what went down next. The "new place" usual for me. The thing is, my last cellmate never told anybody I learned of what he saw, excluding the staff who got him moved. We saw each other from time to time and we'd speak, but that was it. Being on the new block was dry AF, but dry meant things were probably more laid back also, which proved to be the case. I got back into school, got in more talks with my adopted pops, got my G.E.D, as well as some college credit. I also learned how to (and how not to) cut hair.

Things still got real from time to time, but for the most part, I was okay through a slew of cellmates. Then the block changed, got wilder, got worse. And before you knew it, I had words with a guy whose cellmate I hung out with. Next thing I knew, I went from sayin' "my bad" over sitting on the wrong property box, to getting the entire fuck beat outta me.

I went to the health care building so pictures could be taken of how I looked after a clear case of being assaulted. Then I was talkin' to the hole while the people from internal affairs investigated the incident. I was cleared of any trouble and asked if I wanted to press charges. I said no but that I didn't feel safe there anymore and would like a move.

I was held in the intake wings for 30 days before I was packed up and shipped to a minimum-security prison. I'd been down four years now with two to go before I'd be up for parole.

Lincoln

When I got to Lincoln C.C., I was shocked by the lack of fences and how those of us who lived there moved around so freely. I learned later that this was pretty much as "good as it got", outside of actually being free. What I wasn't ready for was the open dorm setting or the open shower, where up to eight people could fit if need be.

I learned there were five housing units. Each unit had two cellblocks. Each cellblock had five dorms. Each dorm held twenty people. I had to get used to this because before this, all I knew were two-person cells. There was also an open bathroom with five toilets, with a lil wall separating each, along with five sinks, mirrors, etc. Really, no privacy, but it was better than I knew before.

Once I got around a little, I started meeting people. What I didn't do this time around was front like I was this super-ganged out person. I was just myself. It definitely felt better 'cause putting on a front takes energy and, in the end, it's not worth it.

Before long, I met someone we'll call "Remy". Remy and I kicked it a bunch, but people were acting funny toward her 'cause she's Trans. I was, too, but since hormones weren't available, I just had to settle with the pretty boy look. Anyway, soon enough, people were all on me for hanging out with Remy. I stayed true to myself and my friend, and didn't give a fuck who said what. The rumor mill started, people were throwin' shade and doin' the whole most. So one day, I walked up to a bunch of the guys who were acting funny. Now, mind you, I knew this could go any way, but I'm the type of person to just get shit over with. So I walked in, and they shut up. I read the room, shit was tense. I took control, and asked questions that allowed anything to go. By the end of the episode, I left no room for doubt or speculation as to who I was, what I liked, and what I was about. After I got done talkin', dudes were clearly stunned at the way I spilled my shit, but all in all, it went over well, and then I went and hung out with Remy.

At twenty-two, I was parked in the zero fucks lane, and I felt good. After a while, there were five of us who were open about ourselves on our block. People looked and talked when we all hung out, but we all just did us. Sometimes we turned the tables on the naysayers and showed them how we could care less about them. We fought hate with positive vibes.

In the midst of all this, I started getting call passes to the law library. I didn't know why, so I just never went. Part of me was scared the pass meant I had some type of new legal issue they could only tell me about there. But I was dumb AF back then, when it came to how things like that worked. Fast forward to now, I know wayyy better, and also the fact that if it was legal drama, ducking the pass wouldn't stop shit from goin' down.

Eventually, my scary ass went over to see what the pass was about. Came to find out, all that fear and pass ducking was for nothing. The pass was just to get me there. The person who made the pass happen was what it was really about. That is how I met Willie Pole.

Willie is the son of Ms. Campbell, who went to the same church as us when I was with the Hammonds. Our families had history and fucked with each other on various levels. Willie's sisters were cool with Chuck, and I was cool with Willie's niece and nephews who were in my age range. Anyway, Willie was about forty years old, so he acted like an uncle to me and told everybody he knew to "look out" for me.

From what I was told, just so happened that Willie's mama and the Hammonds were talking about us, and the conversation went to where we were. Once that came up that we were in the same place. Ms. Campbell told Willie to check for me.

The funniest thing was, I heard about Willie plenty of times as a kid. Mainly because I'd do some hot shit, and my dad would be like, "Keep it up, and you gone end up like Willie." I learned later that my dad used to try and to talk sense into Willie, just like Willie's mom and sisters would when I fucked up early on. I sit and think about how that was the strangest way for life to come full circle back then.

Hmmm. Anyway, Willie worked in the library, and we'd hang out a lot. It didn't hurt that I loved, and still love, to read. So, I'd go over but then I'd go all around and hang with my crowd. Willie was not like us, but he never acted funny toward me for being me.

What was frustrating was that once people connected Willie to me, they would run and tell him shit about me. To me, them telling on me to him was hoe shit, but that didn't stop it from happening. It even got to the point where people were running to Internal Affairs about my lil crowd and the supposed going ons.

Here's the thing, after getting kicked out of Dixon, I was really careful about who I'd get wild with and where we'd get wild. I knew the stories that were told to Internal Affairs weren't true, and people just hated seeing a group of us living our truths and making the most of our situations.

Be that as it may, it wasn't long before our lil crowd was busted up. Remy and I were salty AF but there wasn't shit that could be done.

The good part of the move was I ended up on the same block as Willie, although we were in separate dorms. The weird part was, off jump, dudes were SHADY toward me as soon as I got in the door. This time, though, I was the only one of me around. So, I did me, and held my head up anyway. To this day, I do the same. I look at it as: I am who I am, like me or don't.

****

How It Happened

As I spoke on before, people were steady minding business that wasn't theirs. I started going outside to catch a lil air, and eventually, Remy and I found out we had the same yard schedule. We were attached to the hip every time we popped out, and, yup, we swung a couple episodes like before the move.

One day, we got it poppin and shut the Rec shed off from everybody. We did us and dipped, but soon as we came out of the bathroom attached to the shed, ALL EYES WERE ON US.

Two days later, after niggas ran they mouths, I got called to Internal Affairs. Now, I already expected it 'cause of how the yard was actin'. Willie and I were having a conservation when I was called out. We locked eyes, and that "damn" type feeling came over both us at the same time. We talked a lil more, and I went to talk.

Internal Affairs is the prison equivalent of detectives. Some dudes be so shook about them that these ones acted like this was a real-life episode of "Law and Order". It seemed to me that niggas told them all they could EXCEPT for the fact that I wasn't goin' for none of the tricks they tried.

I wasn't afraid 'cause I knew they couldn't do much by the questions they were asking, the threats they tried, and the way they were wayyyy too thirsty for me to talk. I knew that lying was my only way out, so I lied. Then they tried to tell me that there were cameras that caught me and Remy, but that was a lie. There were no cameras anywhere around, and I looked.

Once they got tired of me, they sent me to the hole under investigation. They ain't have shit so I wasn't worried. Then I heard about Remy.

I came to find out that they got Remy first, and then came for me. Investigations could go up to 30 days before they gotta give up and let you go. Usually, you end up with a ticket which could result in a whooole lotta consequences depending on the charge if you don't beat it at the Adjustment Committee. This was one of the few times any of the put-ons I had worked all the way right. 'Cause I was tough as fuck the entire time the investigation was going,and through countless attempts to make me talk, through the weak ass ticket they put together, and it paid off at the committee.

Two weeks later, Remy and I beat the important half of our ticket. We were "Not Guilty" of the 107: sexual misconduct charge but were found guilty on the unauthorized movement. We ain't give a fuck, though. They was petty AF for the charges any way. We were two consenting adults, and although we didn't admit our guilt of gettin it poppin', we didn't commit a crime. The IDOC just frowned upon sex and made it a rule not to do it.

Now on one side I know why it's a rule. Some people have diseases and won't say so, so it being a rule serves as a deterrent for some. It's in place to keep people safe. On the other side, people gone do what they want, so as long as it's consensual, safe, and not hurting anyone, it shouldn't be that big of a deal.

By the time we got out the hole, the reason we went was twisted and turned a million different ways. None of the stories I heard were accurate. Only me, Remy, and Willie know the truth. Willie only knows 'cause I told him when he came to me after people kept runnin' to him about it. Anyway, I know I had to get used to a whooole new block on a whole new unit.

2 House

No put-ons were needed here. They knew who I was 'cause they saw me around. For the most part, this new dorm I was in was smooth, to say the least. My bunkmate was a dude named Black. He was in his mid-thirties and pretty much seen it all in his time in prison. He had juice in his gang and had it set up that most of the guys in our dorm were in the same gang and from his neighborhood.

The others were wary of being dormed with me until they learned what I was really about beyond the rumors and the obvious. Once the ice was broken, we all kicked it heavy, and before you knew it, I was with them in the gym. First off, working out was not for me. I wanted nooo parts of it. The more the guys tried to get me to, the more I resisted, until I let Black talk me into it.

Now, yeah, I'm clearly a chick. But back then, I was serving Butch Queen vibes 'cause hormone therapy wasn't provided to me for my transition. It was only available to the girls who were already on hormones prior to being incarcerated. Anyway, so, here I go, trying to work out with dudes who looked like they ATE weights for fun...

By the time I hit 24, I was full on hooked to the gym. Black nem were gassin' me up too, and I felt like I couldn't be told shit! Homesick? Lift weights. Problems on the phone? Lift weights. Bored? Lift weights. Back up sexually? Lift weights. Well, I didn't lift weights for that, but I was in the gym faithfully, gettin' my body built how I wanted. I had three months left before my time was up, and I was not fuckin' around.

****

Sadly, I couldn't say the same for everybody. Remy got in trouble again and got shipped out. Jayda left me high and dry. I hadn't talked to Angel in years. My adoptive parents switched up, and told me I couldn't parole there after they'd been tellin' me I could when I'd mention needing a place to go. My sister KEKE moved back from out of town, so since she was back in the state she was option "Y". However, that fell apart too cause **A:** Section 8 wasn't allowing felons to be there. **B:** Felons couldn't be around pit bulls while on parole. **C:** A whole lot I couldn't be around was goin' on over there.

Soooo there was option "Z" — going to a halfway house. It got down to the wire, but it was either violate parole and do my MSR time in jail, and be let out scott-free in 18 months, or ask for halfway house placement and get out on my release day. Shidd… y'all know what I did!

7-20-16

Walking out of prison on parole was one of the best feelings I ever felt. 'Cause parole aside, at least I wasn't in a prison bunk at the end of the night! The thing about parole was, although I was "free", I still had strings attached. Three years' worth. Now the only way my 3 years of parole was getting cut was if I went back in and violated, or if I did so good that I was taken off early. Either way, nothing was poppin till I got through the sixty days of House Arrest that was part of my parole stipulations.

Going into the halfway house was nothing. I just spent six years in worse places. I was at Wayside Cross in Aurora. Everything was new to me in and around the place. Being new, I couldn't help but to read the guys and scan the place like I'd been doing for years. They say "old habits die hard", and I knew it was going to be hard to try and let go of the things I'd learned to get by my time bouncing from place to place, but I was willing to try and start off on the right foot.

Way Side

Wayside was lowkey bussin'. They had a gym room, a computer room, and a nice bathroom up on the living quarters. The whole place was big as fuck, three or four floors if I remember right. The rules were once you get there, you can't leave the grounds for 30 days. You had to attend the church classes and programs. You earned your keep by doing whatever jobs they had in-house (cleaning, sorting donations, picking up donations, working the trucks, or doing somethin' else around there). You couldn't work a real job where you get paid money 'cause if you did, nobody would be there to do those odd jobs there. You also couldn't have a cell phone unless you were on "Level three" or "four". You also couldn't have visits till you were there at least two weeks. Your family could bring you things for you to have, but only after being searched could you have whatever was brought. Then you could only place 3 calls a week. Calls in which the log keeper would dial out and once your people answered, he'd be like, "This is Wayside Cross, so and so would like to talk to you", then you'd get the phone for twenty minutes after who you called told the actual log keeper to give you the phone.

****

I followed the lil rules and played nice, but I had shit to figure out. I was fresh out and broke as fuck. I literally had nothing but the clothes on my back and the lil shit I had in my locker that Keke, Koko and nem got me within a couple days of being free.

It's funny 'cause for all the put=ons I took off, I couldn't, for the life of me, take off the one where I would act like I was okay, even when I clearly wasn't. Regular pride is one thing. You know, being happy you aced a test or hit a goal is one thing too. But foolish pride will have you in your own way and fucked up altogether. This is how that went down.

How It Went Down

Somewhere along the way, between how hectic shit was before I got out, and getting out and seeing how things were, I was salty bout how things went. Hurt, really. So much so that I made up my mind and was like, "Fuck whoever acted funny." I thought I'd "get it on my own" and "wouldn't need anyone".

On top of that was getting through house arrest.

I spent from the time I got out till the beginning of September learning, working, hanging out, trying to keep my head above water, and trying to get a grip. It was during all this that I went into the "T.V. room" one night and noticed that mostly everybody had cellphones. After a bit, I was cool with a nice amount of people in the room, so I'd use theyre phones when I could to refrain from hitting my limit on the halfway house phone. Then, once I passed my first 30 days, I started using my free time to go out within the movement times of my house arrest.

After getting out, I began meeting people who lived around the area, and that was my favorite part. I kinda began seeing around and doing lil shit that people who never been locked up take for granted. I also started making odds and ends by making runs for the new people who couldn't leave the halfway house just yet. Those ends afforded me some lil ways to make the girl I didn't look like on the outside happy. I bought some earrings and dyed my dreadlocks. I still couldn't transition, though. I didn't have the resources, and even if I did, I couldn't do anything till I lost all that muscle. Sure, it looked good, but it wasn't "me". I felt a fraud, a bitch in a muscle suit is how I saw it.

Nevertheless, the show went on. Keke wired me some money one afternoon, and I went and got a lil cellphone. This was fine 'cause, although I didn't have many people to call yet, it made it easier when I made my moves and shit. I also liked being all on Facebook. Getting on social media again was different for me 'cause it'd been a while, and scrolling thru, seeing people who were kids when I went in, accomplishing things, getting apartments, etc., as well as seeing people my age living it up and seeming like they had everything together… Well, to be honest, I felt left behind shit. I was left behind, and that feeling is what I wanted to forget, which led to me going harder on my lil runs.

****

I started filling drug requests from people who couldn't leave the halfway house. I would take the money plus my fee, get what they wanted while I was out and about, and then bring it back to them as I toed the agreement my parole plan stipulated.

After a while, shit went left. One time, I went and got some loud for some guys. They smoked it, and I was talking with them while they did. When I came back into the house for the night, I noticed that EVERYBODY seemed to be staring at me. I wasn't sure why, but I'd find out the next day.

So I did my warehouse job, went outside, came in, and hung out. Next thing you know, Blain, a staff member, called me to his office. Once there, he told me that people said I smelled like weed and I needed to do a piss test for him. I didn't mind 'cause I knew I only did drug requests but I wasn't using.

Imagine my surprise when the test read dirty! Blaine was smiling like he "got me". I was mortified, 'cause a dirty test for me meant (1) Instant Kickout (2) Nowhere to finish my house arrest (3) A call to my P.O (4) Violation of my parole, which brought (5) Prison. Oooohhh no, I wasn't goin' back. So I made a big scene and demanded a new cup 'cause some home kits have been proved faulty.

Blaine and the rest of the staff were TIRED of me. I wore 'em out till they told me ain't no more cups, and the only way to proceed was if I got tested on my own. So I called my dad up and explained the situation. He told me he'd cover the costs for me. I told the staff, and we were off to the hospital so I could be tested for real.

Forty-five minutes later, I was smiling just as hard at Blaine as he was at me all the while poppin' biiiiggg shit about me knowin I was right, fuck him, fuck his broke ass cup, and all that good shit. See, when I'm wrong and tryna get away, I'm good. When I get away, I'm better. But when I was right from the jump, not fuckin' around at all… you can't tell me NOTHINNNN'! The staff was done with me; I was wavin' the hospital results around like Maury told my Baby daddy, "You Are The Father!" So, yeah, I went to sleep with a smile on my face, but it wasn't long before I, in grand fashion, did too much…

Oh Noo

I'm shakin' my head, 'cause looking back, I should've known me actin' bad about me being right was gonna set me up to get nailed for any lil thing. I got kicked out the halfway house for taking a selfie! Yup, tryna be cute got me canned! The selfie itself wasn't the problem, though. It was the fact the picture was of me, in the halfway house bathroom, all in the mirror, shirt off, with the phone all in the reflection of said mirror, Smh… these MFs real life monitor the computers in the computer room 'cause some people who live there can't use 'em 'cause of they cases.

For me, though, that didn't apply, so I was all in that bish. Just like I was still usin' the wall phone for looks, since I had my phone in my pocket I could do whatever with. Back to the story, though…

This time, Felix called me out. The staff sent him 'cause I guess they felt he and I were cool since I talked to him sometimes. Anyway, I got into the side room, and Felix and I are across from each other. He asked me, "Where's your phone?" as if it was a gun. I told him I didn't have one, and that if I had one, I wouldn't be using the wall phone and having the phone log guys call me out.

Felix ain't say shit. He simply reached down and flipped his lil folder open and nodded downward. I followed his motion and came face to face with a paper printout of the post of the selfie I took the night before. I looked back up and locked eyes with Felix. I already knew what it was. He told me I was in violation of the rules and that I could no longer stay there. I tried it all, but there was nothing left to do. I was told I had an hour to pack my things, arrange a ride, and find a place to stay. After the hour, they'd call my P.O and the police, so I can be held till she got there to decide what to do. I ain't know what I was gonna do, but I wasn't gonna go back to prison tonight, not like this, not over a phone, over a rule. So, since it wasn't shit left to deny, I pulled my phone out and made some calls.

****

I called anybody who told me they could help me since I got back, and nobody came through. I was down to my last option, and I tossed my Hail Mary down the field of life. I called SAVAGE. Savage and I know each other from church back in Bolingbrook. We were kids, though, so it didn't count. How well could you really know someone from being shuffled around various church programs?

Anyway, since I'd been free, she and I met, and I thought she was pretty cool. So yeah, I called and once she picked up, I told her what kinda jam I was in. She told me how she had a dude and didn't wanna cause trouble by lettin' me come there. I could respect that. Honesty is always appreciated.

She couldn't help me that way, but she did call around. At one point, she had Willie's mama on the phone tryna help too, but I couldn't go there 'cause Willie was due home soon, and we both couldn't be there as felons on parole.

Finally, we got it together. I had Keke on my cellphone, the parole center on Wayside's phone, and me back forth between both, cryin', tryin' not to go to jail.

Once Keke confirmed to the parole center that I could come there, I was in the clear. I got Leah back on the phone, and she agreed to give me a ride out to Keke's. She pulled up, we pulled off, and that was that…

It's funny, though, 'cause now we both in the car, headed to my sister's, and instead of thinkin' about what was to come, I'm sittin' there taking a minute to really take shorty in. She was two years younger than me, but that meant nothing. We were grown. Yellow skin, like Elle Varner. Pink lips like Ella Mai. Flawless aura, complete package, and she even made pajama pants and a bonnet look good. I don't know what happened 'cause **1**) I don't often like females sexually, and **2**) I'm not shy by a long shot and hadn't been in ages. But something about her had me stuck, speechless, drowned, and fallin' like a lil ass girl over in the passenger seat. I feel funny AF writing this, but shit, if I was gonna write this, I had to keep it a buck! I had to pull it together and snap out of it 'cause we were at Keke's.

Out Dat Jam!

Keke kept it cute… till Savage and I got my bags in. Once I walked Savage out and came back in, Keke went INNN on me. I'm 5ft 5. She comes to my eyebrows, but she had me shook, just like when we were kids. We were always the closest out our family, and everybody knew Keke don't play about me. But it was clear she wasn't bout to play with me neither! Just 'cause I was out that Wayside jam did not mean shit was sweet.

My new situation consisted of me cleaning up the apartment, looking after the dog, job hunting, abiding by my parole, and keepin' shit together in general.

I needed to take baby steps. I knew I was twenty-four, but outside of running away as a teen, this was the first time in ten years that I didn't live in an institution of some sort—prison, Streamwood, group home, halfway house. I found myself at the apartment just sitting there, thinkin' of what my life was up to then, where I was in the moment, and then about what I wanted going forward.

I would use most days applying for a job, ANY JOB! I didn't care what. Keke gave me the couch and some closet space for my things, as well as a shelf in the bathroom. It was fine for the moment, but clearly, this lil setup wasn't gonna be it for me. I always looked to Keke as one would they're mom, but she was only a couple years my senior. That being said, when she told me to get it right and stack my money so I could get a place, I didn't want to disappoint her. I was ready to get my money up.

I had a Lil plan figured out. I had a couple days left on house arrest, but before I could do anything, something just had to go left.

My parole officer told me I couldn't live at Keke's because the house arrest guy who hooked the monitor up told him that he noticed a pitbull in the apartment. Also, 'cause the apartments were Section 8. So now I had to figure something out. Quick. Again.

I asked a few more people I knew, but it didn't look good. As a backup plan, I started looking into homeless shelters that would take a person on house arrest. I found a place called Pacific Garden, and it wasn't very far to get there. I called them, secured a spot, told Keke the deal, and she gave me a ride to the train station. I could tell she was worried before we parted ways. To be honest, I was too. But I put on an "everything's okay" face. I wasn't okay, though. I was headed back to Chicago with nothing but some clothes and a dream.

Uuggghhh

Showing back up in Chicago wasn't bad; I knew what I was up against and how to handle myself. But when I started walking from the Union Station, my "okay" put-on came down hard.

Next thing I know, I'm going down the sidewalk in tears. I was sad. I was frustrated. I was alone. Again.

I checked my phone about a fifth of a way down Canal St. I perked up instantly when I saw Aja's text, sayin' I could use her apartment as a parole site. Although I wondered what changed her mind between her earlier refusals and now, I was in no position to give a fuck. My plan was to get to the shelter, check in, call parole, and switch addresses again. So, my walk got that much easier. What happened next reads like I made it up, but I promise this whole book true AF. Anyway, I texted Aja back, and no more than two more blocks into my trip, a car pulled up about ten feet away.

I would like to say I did some gangsta shit in response to the abrupt way the car stopped, but I can't. I froze up as the window dropped and closed my eyes. This type of shit don't end well, and however I was goin' out, I didn't want to see it, hoping it'd be quick.

Imagine how stupid I looked standin' there eye closed and my face scrunched up for nothing. I opened my eyes at the sound of my birth name being called. I knew that voice, but it'd been years since I heard it.

I looked into the car window and saw Ellis. He was a few years younger than me and was one of the young boys who lived at the house on College St. I couldn't believe it was him, and the timing of it all.

He just happened to be riding by after a run for Lyft and noticed me by my blonde dreadlocks. Once in the car, we kicked it, and he told me what he made of himself after DCFS. I was proud of him. We stopped by a library he knew, and he did me up a resume while I got the exact address from Aja. Ellis and I hung out for another hour or so before he dropped me of at Aja's.

****

No longer in Elgin, Aja spot was on the corner of 91st and Cottage Grove, above the 123 Mini Mart. I'd never lived in this part of Chicago, so I was once again new somewhere. Aja gave me the rundown, and then I called the parole center to check in. It felt good to be able to breathe easy, knowing I had a place. But it wasn't the two seconds before Aja and her dude got into an argument about me staying there.

Meanwhile, my new parole officer showed up. At first, she didn't believe I was who I said I was. I guess how I read on paper gave her a different picture of who I might've been in her mind. I don't know. What I do know is her face was priceless when I told her Aja is my mom and where I was staying.

She clearly didn't know what to do, but she tried her best to hold herself together. She gave me her expectations of me, lettin' me know to call in once a week and meet her face-to-face sometime in the first week of every month. When I went to let her out, I let her know I caught the look she had, and knew what she thought, but that I just needed a chance to get myself together. She smiled and reminded me to follow what she asked before goin' about her way.

I got back to the apartment, and Aja explained I couldn't stay after all, but could continue to use the address with my P.O. I called Keke and told her. She told me how she ain't want me out there like that. So, before it was all said and done that night, the plan was set that I'd stay on cottage when I needed to check in, but I'd actually live with Keke nem at the other apartment.

Out Dat Jam Again

Whew Chile! It was a lot, but we made it work. Things were going smoothly, but I was still broke. I didn't know much of anything about the immediate area, so I started going outside to see what was around in Willowbrook.

Back to those put-ons, I didn't have many, but I was playin' up the pretty boy shit. I was out one day, and noticed a McDonald's right outside the apartment complex. I knew nothing about fast food, but I wanted in. I was broke AF, wearing summer clothes when it was clearly fall. So I walked in McDonald's twice a day for a month, and I talked to anyone I could until they gave me a shot.

In between trying for a job and landing one, I met someone. We were cool at first, then grew into more.

Toya and I were with each other day in and day out to the point that pretty soon I met her mom, saw where she lived, and was introduced to her friends. I always went to her place, but she never came to where I lived. I wasn't ashamed of her. I just felt funny 'cause Keke's spot was a one bedroom meant for two people, but housed her, her guy, the dog, me, and her guy's cousin or bro when they came to hang out or just needed to crash. What was I supposed to do? Bring her over like, "Aye, shorty, this my couch! I use it as a bed, and the front space is my room when nobody's around?" So I kept going over to her place till one day I showed her how I lived. Her mom and she were basically roommates and split the bills over at they spot. They had a lot of room, though. So before I knew it, Toya told me they made the basement up like a lil place and told me I could live there, and we'd all share the common spaces and split the bills three ways. I agreed and signed the lease agreement that was drawn up for me.

I now had a job and my own space to live. I felt things finally were coming together.

****

McDonald's was okay, but I was a fish out of water. I was not used to this. What I really wasn't used to was taxes! Ooohhwee, I was on fire when I got my lil pay. I just knew I had put a million hours in! So, I went from home into work and showed my BLACK ASS! After my boss broke down how taxes work and assured me there was no error in my pay, I took the same black ass and had several seats. There was a lot I didn't know about, regarding how to do things in the "legal" way. I'd never been a part of the legal workforce. My favorite part of the job was meeting people and talkin' shit. It seemed better to try and make someone smile during the job than to be moody or dry acting. It doesn't cost to be kind. Years later, I'd watch Maya Angelou have a talk with Oprah, and what stuck with me was how she said, "Nobody will remember everything you said. Nobody will remember everything you did. But everybody will always remember how you made them feel." It was heavy to hear, and I try to keep it in mind now. But at this part of my story, well, I wasn't there yet. I felt behind in life, and before long, anything went...

The thing about money is, once you get some, you want more, and the chase gets addicting. So much so that you will do the absolute most to get it. Just like a hype to they're drug of choice, to the money, I was hooked.

I came from nothing, so when I had something, I wanted to keep it rolling. I never wanted to feel what I felt when I was dead broke again. I would work, and I would do a lil somethin' on the side, once my side shit took off, McDonald's seemed like I didn't need it, but I stayed. It gave me a good excuse when my parole officer asked questions about how I spent my time.

But then, I got fired. All I knew was I'm doin' iight, but now, as I said before, all bets were off.

Trapaholic

This is the part where I give y'all a rundown of how I did things, what I made from it, how lit shit was, and all kind of whatever. Well, y'all know where I'm writing from, so lemme just say that I meant it when I said all bets were off. That being said, I can't give y'all the real without mentioning the people I got it in with. The details are what make the story. But I can't let me writing this put others within the reach of the long arm of the law, plus, this not that kind of book. But since you read this far, I won't leave y'all out without answers.

- Drug dealing
- Credit fraud
- Prostitution
- Armed robbery

These things were part of what brought in the money. These things were subject to go down at any given time. The only time when I wasn't lining a move up was when I had to do my parole officers check-ins. Soon as she got back in her unmarked and pulled off, I went back in mode. The highs were high, the lows were low, but none of it matters now 'cause all I have left are the memories. Once I was indicted and everything fell apart, I cried like a baby 'cause I knew I was through. This was a jam there was no getting out of.

Do Not Pass Go... Smh

Damn... I was back in jail... I let everybody down... I let me down... I had a chance... I blew it. The only way to go was up from here. I was at rock bottom. Nothing glitzy or glamourous about facing charges. I got arraigned. I plead not guilty. I went to countless court dates and attorney visits, needing a way out. I got all the evidence presented to me. Got in the law library and learned what I needed to write up motions. Set up for trail. Over the next year, in between setting for trial and going, I was told by attorneys that deals were on the table. I wasn't interested but I was curious. When I was told I faced 75 years for my first two charges and 45 for the third, I just had to know what was considered a deal. My attorney said 30 years at 85%, meaning I had to do whatever 85% of 30 years came out to. He said it as cool as one would ask somebody what the weather was supposed to be. I cussed his ass out and went to my cell. Trail was my only option.

The day of trail, I was nervous but I put on my "I'm okay" face. As for the put-ons from earlier in life, Whew Chile... they had to go mostly. So I'm in the side room, ready for the usual attorney/client talk before the proceedings get underway. Jury selection was what I was told was first on our list. I found it funny how the lawyers always said "we, we, we," but if shit went wrong, they'd go home. I'd go to prison.

Anyways, we met, we talked. Shit took a hard turn left. So much so that by the middle of the court session, it was clear I was going down, fast. So after a sidebar and coming to a conclusion, we pulled. I pulled out of trial and took 21 years at 50%, meaning I just signed the next 10 ½ years of my life away. This is the downside of all that fly-ass-get-money shit. And it hit different for me because I know what prison is like. But two weeks later I went to Statesville, and two months after that, I found out hell had side rooms.

Pinckneyville

AAAWW yeah. I.fucked.up.bigggg. This made Shawnee look like daycare. All that was good was we had two times the cellblock was open instead of just one. I hour the first round, 45 minutes the second round, "top floor-bottom floor" style.

As I've said plenty so far, I was once again "new" somewhere. But I knew what prisons are made of, and I'd grown tired of who I'd been and how I handled things at different points in life. So outside of being wary of the people on the block, I came through the door simply being me, no put-ons.

I had served a year in county, so once I touched here, I had basically 9 ½ years left. Just knowing it was a lot, but I learned it was plenty people who would've LOVED to have my time.

Funny thing about life is, no matter how you grow or where you go, pieces of your past show up. I ran into people from the streets as well as different prisons I'd been to years ago. Some left and come back, and some never got free but just transferred from place to place. In the midst of it all, I "settled in" and got into the swing of things.

One day, I was in the line headed somewhere with the rest of the cellblock. At some point, our line crossed with another line, and I saw a familiar face. We weren't friends, but we weren't "into it" either. It was P.J, and he was at Lincoln when I was there. We locked eyes and gave that "Wassup" type nod and kept on our ways. I noticed he knew a couple dudes in my line too. Anyway, a few days later, I was up doin' my daily thing. When I came to the block from my room, I couldn't help but notice that the vibes were off. I caught the looks, I saw the subtle nods from one to another. It was when I walked toward the back of the top floor that I confirmed I wasn't trippin', and the vibes were meant for me.

As I spoke to someone I kicked it with, I heard someone say to they homie a few feet away, "Yeah, they say that MF got put in the hole for fuckin'." I glanced over, and sure enough, they were talking and burning a hole in the side of my face all the while. That's when it clicked. P.J knew them. I saw them talkin' in line that day. If I were the younger me, I would've addressed them, but I didn't. I didn't have shit to hide or to prove. So I pretended I ain't hear. Besides, they got the story half right, I did go to "Seg", "The Hole" back then. It just didn't play out how everyone thought it might. Remy and I beat the sex part in true jail fashion, although who I am and what I'm about spread like wildfire. It came to the point that if someone asked if it was true, I spilled the tea with no filter. If the story would be told, it would be told right!

Pinckneyville has many names, but I liked and still like to call it Freaknyville. It's a whooole lot of actin' bad poppin' off in all 6 of the buildings; there was receiving, then once you got out that building, you were headed to one of five housing units. This was pretty much the only place I went to where those of us in the LGBTQT+ community were the majority, as opposed to the minority.

I still was butchy AF, but there were soooo many girls down there doin' them. I would chill and hang out with some, wishing I could transition, but things were still unavailable to us who weren't on hormones prior to arriving. I thought about what led to me being here and kicked myself. I blew through money like water out there, and while I was out wildin', my transition was put on the back burner. "I should've done it then" is what I would say, but then I'd think of how I got all swollen and understood that wasn't gonna work either. I was out to have a seamless transition, not to be clocky AF, serving holiday heart vibes!

****

I was now 26, and I figured if I couldn't get hormones, then I' ma do what I can without 'em. So I began the process of making myself lose the muscle I had worked for back when I was around Black and the guys.

Meanwhile, I had a cellmate named Josh, and we were cellies for a couple of months. He and I were cool, but we weren't fuckin'. He was more like the brotherly type in my eyes. After a while, I learned he wanted to write books. I wasn't into it at the time, but I loved to read and was interested in seeing Josh accomplish his goal. I'd read chapters and rough drafts, letting him know my honest opinion. Three weeks later, he had his goal hit. A week after that, he went to the hole for talkin shit to a guard, but he would be okay since he only had a couple weeks left on his parole time.

As I sit and think, my time with Josh showed me the inside look into how to to get a book written in prison. Writing it was the easy part. The business side would prove to be hard but not impossible. The saying goes that people come into your life for a reason, a season, or a life time. Seeing how Josh did his thing gave me the confidence to believe I could do the same.

After Josh, I got moved around on the block a couple of times before placement decided to move me to another housing unit and cellblock.

I wasn't acting a role. I was just being me. I was reminded of how bumpy the road of being myself could be. My next cellmate was a fuckin' clown. Simple and plain. We didn't mix through the door. I tried, but he was impossible. He only had a year left on his time but was so immersed in jail shit that he acted like he had life to do, meaning his outlook on life was bleak and he only thought about the small picture. He was always downing somebody, actin' tough, sneak dissin' on the LGBTQ+ community. I wasn't goin', so I checked his ass like the bold bish I am. Eventually, he tried me. Once he put his hands on me, I got busy. Locked in the cell, nobody could save you but yourself. I was no Clarissa Shields, but I wasn't a slouch either. I hated fighting and only did that type of shit if I have to. Keith was my cellmate about a week longer, then it happened again, and he had to go. So he packed his things and had the guards move him. I didn't care where he went, he just couldn't stay with me no more.

I didn't really come out the cell much, but once I popped out a lil, I met people on the block like me. I loved when I'd meet community members who were cool. Soon enough, though, I was actin' BAD. Once I let my hair down and learned more of the block, I was havin' company in my room, being company in someone's room, smokin', and generally makin' the most. Tryin' to vibe out with my crowd.

The Rub

Soon enough, shit got fucked up, though. A girl named Shay and I were cool as fuck, and we were in my room. My new cellmate, Donny, was chill, and was the complete opposite of Keith. So when he wanted the room, or I wanted the room, we'd give each other time. Anyway, Shay and I were just chillin'. Somebody told a guard; the guard came and left but returned with more officers. Shay and I went to the hole. We were not supposed to room hop, so I figured we'd go down for a couple of weeks for unauthorized movement.

The way it happened didn't sit right. I knew Donny ain't tell 'cause he'd been the lookout plenty of times when I had company over. When the guard came by, he'd walk by with the code word, and me and whoever would make like nothin' was up. I learned later that Relly told the guard Shay and I were fuckin', so the guard took his word and pulled up. But at the time, I was just shocked we got put in the hole for hanging out. When the guard pulled up, we were really not doin' shit.

So I get in the hole, and the next day, I got my write-up. Here was different than Lincoln, and I couldn't yell to Shay since she was on a whole another cellblock. There were two cellblocks used for the hole.

We were wrote-up for… you guessed it: sexual misconduct. I was no stranger to write-ups, but I wasn't goin' for this! The whole ticket was a lie. I told the Adjustment Committee the deal, but c'mon, they hear it all every day. So, they found us guilty and gave us two months in segregation and added 30 days to our sentences. I couldn't take it, not for a ticket we really didn't do.

The ticket said that when night yard opened, the guard saw Shay leave her cell and come in mine. And upon following her, he walked up to see her giving oral favors.

First off, that wasn't true. Second off, "oral favors" isn't specific. Third, the cameras at the back of the block would show the true story. As I said before, the guard came, left, and came back. If he saw anything, he would've stayed on the spot and would've radioed for the other officers to put us in handcuffs and take us to the hole.

Also, he lied about how Shay got into my room. This is chess not checkers, and I had company enough to know how to get away with it. Shay came into my room after dinner and locked in. I was already in my room, and Donny was in the room too. We had an hour before night yard, so we would chill. When yard time came, Donny would leave, we'll get it poppin', and by the time night yard was over, the cell block would've opened, and Shay and I would've left the room and hung out on the block as usual. All three of us were in the room when the guard came and asked as our ID numbers. However, the door was closed, and Shay was sitting in the chair by the door literally right under the screen, out of view. Donny and I recited our numbers to assure the guard we were the two who lived there. Then the guard left.

I found out later that Relly had told right after dinner when he saw Shay slide.

Anyway, night yard happened, Donny left, we stayed, but we weren't doin' shit. The guard askin' Donny and me for our numbers threw me off. We only stayed at that point because I was sure the cell was being watched, especially after seeing we were the only cell the guard came to. Waiting till the block busted was the best bet. That is if Relly hadn't told. Then, the guard pulled back up with help. He bust the door down. Nothing was happening, but we went to the hole after being questioned as to why Shay was in my room. If what the ticket said was true, they wouldn't have had to ask. I eventually got in touch with Shay and confirmed she got slammed on the ticket too. We kept in touch, and I wrote a grievance to the warden.

Fighting The Good Fight

Writing a grievance was tricky more because it set you up for possible, and here, well, very likely retaliation from whoever you wrote up. It was the only way, though. I wasn't caring bout shit but that extra 30 days, though. I wasn't taking it. Not off a lie.

I wrote the warden and labeled the grievance as an emergency, so I know it'd get into the right hands. I explained it all, exposing the real and also highlighting the cameras which could be pulled up to prove the truth.

By the time I got relief, we'd BEEN out the hole and had our privileges back. And to make it better, I got a notice in the mail sayin' that the warden put my release day back where it was supposed to be. From then on, I was mindful of the guards AND the other people around me, as they were not playin' fair at all.

****

Before that phony-ass ticket, I'd gotten two petty tickets. The first 'cause I forgot my ID in my room. The second because the TV I bought didn't work, and they wouldn't replace it. So, I had someone fix it for a fee on a "shake down". The guard took my TV and wrote me up because my TV was now "altered" due to the security tape being removed in the process of it being fixed. I had to destroy it and buy another TV. After I caught the ticket for the phony shit, I got two write–ups. One 'cause one of my cellmate had contraband in our room, but that ticket was expunged 'cause he went home by the time the Adjustment Committee called for us. Then, I caught one for refusing housing.

Jan 6th 2020

I refused housing for my own safety. After getting out the hole with Shay, I'd been placed back on the same block we were moved from. In the two months we were in the hole, a lot of moves happened around the prison. When I got back, there were more of the community there, and we stuck together. My closest friend was a girl named Monica, and we were real life kickin' it. Kita, B. fly, Sparkle and Gabby, Shay and I saw each other from time to time, even though she was in a different block with some other girls.

Anyway, on January 6th, I was told to pack my things and that I was going one block over. At this point, I'd had fifteen cellmates, and shit didn't always go well. A girl like me had to be careful about who I lived with. So, I packed my things, said 'my see you laters', and hcadcd to the next block over. I only knew that I didn't know anybody over there.

I got there and went to the ccll. I looked in and was glad it was empty, so nobody could tell me I couldn't move in there with them. I didn't have to worry.

I began setting up my things when the lock popped. I poked my head out the door because sometimes the guard pops your lock from the control center if there's somewhere you've been called to be or just to get your attention.

My gut sank when I looked down the way and saw this big, ugly mf named Cam walkin' with his mattress. I didn't even have to say shit; he knew off rip who I was. His guys told him when he was yellin' to them when he came over. I didn't know his guys, but they knew me by sight and rumors.

I was nervous but decided to give him a fair shot. Then the doors popped open, and the cellblock was now open. The vibe was off, so I texted Savage and let her know I had a funny feeling. Then I just stood around and pretended I didn't see Cam and his boys all bunched up, glancing my way as they talked. I couldn't do nothin' with a group of big dudes, so I figured if somethin' bout to happen out here, at least the camera would catch it.

Nothing happened, though. I went back into the cell, and Cam did too. That's when shit went left. He told me how he don't fuck with my kind, how his boys said to beat me up, yadda, yadda, yadda. I'm small but I sized him up. I couldn't do nothin' with him, and wasn't about to try. He was talkin' aggressively, but he didn't touch me. I wasn't bout to stick around to give him a chance to. I had nothin' to prove! Shiiit. I like myself better with the fuck not beat out me. I told him I'd leave, and when my block opened for lunch, I left. The guard tried to talk me into staying, and I said I wasn't safe. He threatened me with the hole. I didn't care. I'd rather be in the hole, safe in trouble, than out of trouble and hurt if I went back in that room. I stood firm and refused. It was what it was.

I didn't end up in the hole after all, but I was put in the receiving building on the back strip with a ticket. I didn't care, and my loved ones didn't either; they were just glad I stood up for myself and was safe. On the phone, I also mentioned how I was sure a loss of privileges was gonna be my consequence. I got a month loss of privileges and two weeks of room restriction where you only allowed to come out ya room to shower.

Before my ticket got heard I had access to the receiving yard. A couple time a week, I didn't really fuck with people who weren't part of the community, but I talked to a couple of guys who were on the back wing too. It was awkward for me at first, but then it got easier.

Since I'd been on 6B, I'd been writing mental health and healthcare to see what I could get done as far as getting on hormones. Trying paid off 'cause eventually, I saw Mrs. Mason, a chocolate–colored, no shit taking lady with a "don't play with me" attitude.

We were having a conversation at first, but then the questions she was asking led me to understand this wasn't a casual meeting; this was an evaluation. By the end of our meeting, she said she'd do what she could to help me on hormones. I was happy because had I not believed Monica when she told me the girls did a lawsuit and they looked like they were winning wherever they were, I wouldn't't've had the info I needed to get help that D.O.C was now even grudgingly offering. Ms. Mason also signed me up for groups.

My time on the back row closed, and I was now put on 1C in 73 cell. The moment I hit the block, it came alive, but as I tuned everything out and kept it pushin', I realized the room was occupied. I called him to the door and explained my situation. He was like, "So, come in," and I did.

Although he let me in, I was on alert. I was only on alert because when shit goes a lil too smoothly, with a cellmate situation one of four things is bout to happen:

1. He tryna get his dick wet and is overly friendly.
2. He's on the down-low and just as nervous as you.
3. He wanna rob you or try to finnese you out whatever you have.
4. He's genuinely just a cool person who understands that just because a person is different doesn't make them less then. Number four is rare to run into, but sometimes you luck up.

We kicked it, but I could tell by the questions he was asking that he wanted to see if he could get some. I played like I was dumb and let the slick shit he was poppin' fall flat. Yeah, I like to fuck, but I'm not friendly like that. I knew him for all of a New York minute, and he tryna play. "No, thank you".

Once his guys saw me, it was over with for him. The gang he was in wasn't going and told him he had to put me out or he had to leave, or they was gonna fuck him up for lettin' me come in the first place.

He was cool as he explained how shit was about to go. I asked him what he was about to do and he said, "Leave."

So he packed up and left. I was alone, but I liked alone. It meant I was safe.

#17 The Worst

A few days after the other boy left, I got a new one. He was my seventeenth cellmate. When he came through, I didn't care if he stayed or went. I'd been in Freaknyville for sixteen months, and I didn't put much into dudes, really. I had no "put-ons", but they all had 'em on for the most part. I told him soon as he came to the door, "Aye look, obviously I'm different, but I ain't on shit. You can leave now or stay if you want, but if you stay, shit gonna be reeeaaall different for you. They gonna test you, they gone talk about you, blah, blah, blah."

He looked at me and was like, "Cool, help me get my locker up here."

Exactly as I told him would happen, it happened. But he still ain't leave. We were cellmates for a lil under two weeks, and we did our shit. His name was Lil Joe. So right before the two-week mark, I came back in from runnin' around with Shay, and Lil Joe got to tellin' me how he bothered by how people treating him, how his homie from his hood looked at him differently for being in my room, and how I acted like I'm too good for him, and whateva. Look, he spilled his tea to me a few days in. He was in a gang, so he ain't want me to tell his business. He was cute, but I wasn't on that type of time with him. I shut that shit he was talking down 'cause I reminded him that I had told him what to expect. Next thing you know, he punched me, and I tasted blood. It happened so fast I had to take a second and switch gears. I knew it was real when he hit me again and got to beatin' my ass, talking bout how I had a smart mouth and he was bout to put me in my place.

His punches hurt, but I thugged it out and gave him the business. A fight was a fight, but once he got to get the upper hand, he got to pulling at my shorts. At first, I thought he was tryin' to grab me and gain leverage, but once I understood he was about to take me, I fought a whole nother fight. My face was swelling, my lip was busted, and my nose was leaking blood all over us and the room. He didn't care. I tried to get to my razor, but he got wind of it and beat me more. I tried to get to the emergency button, but he kept pullin' me, punchin' me, and draggin' me to the backside of the room. I yelled for help, but nobody came. We were on lockdown for the night. That's how I ended up back on the block after runnin' around with the other girls. My neighbor heard the commotion but instead of helping, he was listening, laughing, and broadcasting what was going on to the rest of the block. EVERYBODY heard. EVERYBODY knew. Nobody helped me. He beat the fuck out me and had his way with me. My soul hurt, my body hurt, and my scalp hurt from the grip he had on my hair as he was punchin' me in between tryin' to force his musty ass dick past my lips when he was doin' me dirty. I wanted to cry. I begged him to stop. I did all I could. This was February 2nd, 2020. It's now October 2021, and I can still feel the pain, hear the laughs, taste the blood, and remember the small way I felt that night into the morning as the block buzzed, and people were making jokes openly about the pleas they heard. This was not my first time being hurt in a place, but I had never been done as dirty and beaten as badly as I was when "Lil Joe-Joe Milton" decided to take what I didn't give him. I winced in pain when I walked. I wasn't okay. I wanted to kill him, but I didn't want to catch a life sentence. The guards came 'cause somebody told them that Lil Joe and I had fought. I told a guard what had really happened in that room, but he fumbled completely and mishandled everything. It took me writing to my loved ones and them blowing up the higher–ups' phones up for me to get help. A month and a week after, I was transferred out and sent to another medium-maximum prison.

Western Illinois C.C.

After Freaknyville, it took me about a year to open up and let people who live on the block here try to hang out with me. I'm different in all the right ways. I've been here since March 2020. Fresh off the van, niggas was on dirt with me. Even on the van, niggas was whispering about the way I look. I still wasn't on hormones, but I did what I could to keep it together. I don't try to look good for nobody; I just like to be presentable. I feel my best when I take that extra time to groom in the mornings.

When I got here, I wouldn't get in the shower. I didn't want to be hurt if somebody caught me naked. So, I washed up in my room till I got a pass to shower in private at health care every night. My first cellmate was okay, but then he offered me sex. I turned him down, and things were awkward. Then he tried to make me leave. I told him that he wasn't tryin' to make me leave when he was offering sex to me, and if one of us was leaving, it was gonna be him. I wasn't acting tough; I was just tired of how dudes act in prison toward me. He left, and I took the time to cry, decompress, and really focus on me.

As I said before, it took about after a year after Freaknyville for me to open up with people. If you saw me now for the first time, you would never guess what my path was like to get to where I am now. I'm still in prison, but I'm at a point in my life where I love the fuck outta me and accept me. I do what works for me, and I'm unapologetically me. I walk pretty with my head held high every day, and I don't give a fuck who likes me or don't like me. I catch the shade, but it don't block my shine! I've now been in talks with therapists, psychologists, doctors, and nurses consistently since I got here 19 months ago. I was finally able to start hormone therapy 16 months ago, and I'm in what I like to call "puberty 2.0". It's been a wild ride, but the results bring a smile to my lips and a tear to my eyes. I'm on my way! I shower alone after having had 5 cellmates here, and I live alone (for now). I'm loved by those who love me, and I kick it with a few dudes who like Savage, keep me smiling. There's been a few big wins for the Trans community that I'm proud to be a part of. I help when I can and fall back when I need to.

Last word 10-27-21

Don't get it fucked up, though. Every day is not rainbows and sunshine. On those days, I take time to myself and get my vibes all the way together. When people try me, I let it fly, check a MF, or read them in the sweetest way possible. It takes a lot to be humble, but I can't let anyone get me to the point where I'm willing to fuck up what I have going on. I have nothing to prove, and I have nothing to hide. Between March and October, I set this book aside because the feelings were intense. But I got back to it a couple weeks ago. I wanted to finish what I started. Maybe my journey to now will help someone see that life is too heavy with put–ons on top. It's funny how to be who I am, I had to lose who I was. Strippin' the put-ons saved me from myself!